Best
Practices

The Model
Employee Handbook
for California
Nonprofits

MANAGEMENT CENTER

Helping good causes since 1977

This handbook has been made possible by grants from The David and Lucile Packard Foundation and The James Irvine Foundation.

PUBLISHERS
Jossey-Bass Inc.

The Management Center,
Robert Walker,
Executive Director

AUTHOR
Leyna Bernstein

GRAPHIC DESIGN
Evangeline Welch,
Design Write!

Best Practices: The Model Employee Handbook for California Nonprofits could not have been created without suggestions and sample policies provided by The Management Center's nonprofit clients. In particular, we would like to thank the following organizations for lending us copies of their own employee handbooks:

Affordable Housing Associates
Alzheimer's Association, Bay Area
The American Red Cross
Battered Women's Alternatives
Big Brothers/Big Sisters of the East Bay, Inc.
California Association of Local Arts Agencies
California Chamber of Commerce
The Family Violence Prevention Fund
Golden Gate Community, Inc.
Mid-Peninsula Management Corporation
The NAMES Project
SeniorNet
The Women's Philharmonic

About *Best Practices: The Model Employee Handbook for California Nonprofits*

In our work with nonprofits throughout Northern California, we on the consulting staff of The Management Center often receive requests for assistance in crafting and communicating personnel policies. ***Best Practices: The Model Employee Handbook for California Nonprofits*** is one way in which we are responding to this need in the nonprofit community.

You can use our handbook as a step-by-step guide for creating your own, or use specific sections to update existing policies and identify new ones. We hope that you will also use this handbook to gain insight into why certain policies are needed and to broaden your knowledge of personnel practices.

The handbook has been designed to inspire you to write personnel policies in language that best reflects your organization's mission and work culture. We caution you not to use language taken directly from handbooks from other sources (such as employee handbooks from the private sector or those written to comply with union contracts) without first tailoring the policies and wording to reflect the environment within your organization.

This is the first edition of ***Best Practices***. We expect to update and expand this handbook continually as we work with our clients and gain additional knowledge about the personnel policy needs of nonprofits.

We welcome your comments and suggestions and have included a feedback sheet in the back of this handbook for this purpose.

This handbook, or any part thereof, may not be reproduced, except for use within your organization, without the written permission of The Management Center.

A Word or Two about the Law

It is critical that you have your own handbook reviewed by a qualified employment attorney before it is printed and distributed.

Many of the policies contained in this handbook address complex legal issues, and the only way to be certain you are adequately covering your specific obligations is to consult with your own legal counsel. (The Management Center can provide you with a referral to an employment attorney specializing in nonprofits.)

Your goal should be to satisfy your organization's risk management needs while providing a set of sensible, humane workplace policies.

Neither the print nor the electronic edition of **Best Practices: The Model Employee Handbook for California Nonprofits** *is intended to be a substitute for experienced legal advice. Although we have attempted to cover most major issues regarding recent employment and labor law, the handbook is not all-inclusive. The information it provides is general in nature; the materials are exemplars only. This publication is not a do-it-yourself guide. The Management Center, Jossey-Bass and its associates do not guarantee the applicability of these materials to your specific organizational needs. Laws are subject to change at any time and legal requirements vary from jurisdiction to jurisdiction. Nothing herein should be relied upon without a full legal review of your organizational circumstances, as well as the laws of the operative jurisdiction. If you need warranted legal advice, see an attorney.*

How to Use This Handbook

1.
AS A TEMPLATE:

This handbook is designed to be used as a template or guide for creating your own personnel policy handbook. The order the policies appear in here is the order that we suggest you follow in your own handbook. Certainly there is no one right way to produce a personnel policy handbook, and you may modify, delete or rearrange policies to suit your needs.

2.
TO UPDATE EXISTING POLICIES:

Scan this handbook for policies that are missing from your own. Pay particular attention to policies that are marked with this symbol:

It means that the policy is **required by or related to a state or federal labor law.**

3.
TO ENHANCE EXISTING POLICIES:

Even if your own personnel policy handbook is up to date, you can find ideas here for improving communication of information, adding innovative practices or rearranging the format of your handbook. Look for this symbol:

It indicates **creative or innovative** policies.

Suggestions about Format

- On the enclosed computer disk, you will find text files of *Best Practices'* sample policies. You may use, edit, copy and distribute these policies within your agency only. All copy right and credit information must remain intact. Any further distribution, in print or electronic formats, is strictly prohibited.

- Distribute your handbook in a three-ring binder, so that you can add and delete pages without needing to reprint your entire document.

- Date each page in your handbook, so that you can identify when a policy was last updated, changed or added. Retain copies of old policies for your records and keep track of when policy changes are made.

- Provide samples of frequently used personnel forms, such as your performance evaluation, change of status and corrective action forms.

- Include an acknowledgment page that is signed, dated and returned by the employee, and placed in his or her personnel file. The acknowledgment form should be at the back of the handbook and should indicate that the employee has read its contents.

- Create an appendix in addition to your table of contents, to help employees find a policy based on key words, even if they don't know its formal name.

About Sample Policies

Most of the sample policies in this handbook are offered in three versions. Each version is tailored to a different fictitious nonprofit organization. All three are described at right. Occasionally one sample will apply equally to two or three organizations.

You occasionally will see a sample policy for Leading Edge Agency only, because it has the resources and staff to implement more personnel policies than the other, smaller organizations.

While these organizations differ in size and workplace culture, we encourage you to read all the policies of the three agencies and to select policies from any of them, depending on which best suits your needs. Never put a new policy into place without being sure that you can follow through on it consistently. Many organizations get into trouble by publishing policies they cannot support due to time, budget or staffing constraints.

Creative Agency

A nonprofit with a small staff (8 employees) and an informal, team-oriented environment. Personnel policies and human resources practices are managed by the executive director.

By the Book Agency

BBA

A medium-sized nonprofit (27 employees) with a long history and a professional, structured work environment. Personnel policies and human resources practices are managed by the director of operations and/or the office manager.

Leading Edge Agency

A large nonprofit (130 employees) with a reputation for being innovative and for committing to an internal environment that mirrors the values of its external service mission. Personnel policies and human resources practices are managed by the director of human resources. Human resources assistance to employees is provided by the director of human resources and a two-person staff.

Welcome...

Creative Agency

Welcome to Creative Agency! We believe that outstanding people are the key to our success. Through the efforts of our staff members, Creative Agency has established itself as a leading organization in our community. To ensure our continued success, we feel it is important that all staff members understand our policies and procedures. This handbook is intended to help familiarize you with them. We encourage you to use this handbook as a valuable resource for understanding our organization.

If you have any questions, please do not hesitate to ask either your manager or any member of our management team.

My best wishes to you, and thank you for taking this first step in getting to know Creative Agency.

Allison Attagirl, Executive Director

By the Book Agency

Welcome. It is our pleasure to welcome you as a member of the staff of By the Book Agency. You are an integral part of a dynamic nonprofit organization.

As an employee of By the Book Agency, you are a community relations representative both on and off the job. We ask that you learn about our organization so that you can speak confidently about By the Book Agency in all your associations.

We designed this manual to help you understand what your benefits are, and what policies guide your day-to-day activities here at By the Book Agency.

We think working with By the Book Agency is a special opportunity. We hope that you will find your employment a matter of both pride and satisfaction, and that it will be mutually productive and enjoyable.

Sincerely,

Donald Dogooder
Executive Director

Carrie Conscientious
Board President

Author's Comments

Begin your handbook with a statement of welcome signed by the executive director and, perhaps, the board chair. The first few pages that an employee sees should be a positive reflection of your organization's culture and values.

Welcome, continued

Leading Edge Agency

Welcome! Leading Edge Agency is a special organization made up of people who work together to affirm our connection to humanity and to serve the community we all share. We strive to operate in a work environment that is marked by honest, responsible and sincere human interaction. As a team, our aim is to support each other in achieving individual and organizational goals.

This handbook serves as a guide for working together. Further, it outlines Leading Edge Agency's commitments to our employees and the commitments we expect in return. Please read it carefully, and use it as you need. If we live our shared values daily, and if we follow these stated guidelines, we will all enjoy an exceptional working environment.

Sarah Striver, Executive Director

Equal Employment Opportunity

Creative Agency

We maintain a strong policy of equal employment opportunity. We seek to achieve equal opportunity for all staff members as articulated by federal, state and local laws. Creative Agency actively seeks to recruit individuals without regard to race, creed, color, gender, sexual orientation, disability, marital status, veteran status, national origin, age or physical handicap. Our equal employment opportunity philosophy applies to all aspects of employment, including recruitment, training, promotion, transfer, job benefits, pay and dismissal.

By the Book Agency

BBA

It is the policy of this agency to afford equal opportunity, in all aspects of employment, to all persons without discrimination on the basis of race, religion, sex, national origin, ethnicity, age, physical disabilities, political affiliation, sexual orientation, color, marital status or medical condition. This policy shall apply to all employees, applicants for employment, board and committee members and volunteers, and extends to all phases of employment, including recruitment, screening, referral, hiring, training, promotion, discharge or layoff, rehiring, compensation and benefits.

Leading Edge Agency

(LEA)

WORKPLACE DIVERSITY
We cultivate a work environment that encourages fairness, teamwork and respect among all employees. We are firmly committed to maintaining a work atmosphere in which people of diverse backgrounds and lifestyles may grow personally and professionally.

EQUAL EMPLOYMENT OPPORTUNITY
Leading Edge Agency is an equal opportunity employer. It is our strong belief that equal opportunity for all employees is central to the continuing success of our organization. We will not discriminate against an employee or applicant for employment because of race, religion, sex, national origin, ethnicity, age, physical disabilities, political affiliation, sexual orientation, color, marital status, veteran status or medical condition (i.e., AIDS or ARC-related or cancer) in hiring, promoting, demoting, training, benefits, transfers, layoffs, terminations, recommendations, rates of pay or other forms of compensation. Opportunity is provided to all employees based on qualifications and job requirements.

Author's Comments

By putting these policies at the beginning of your handbook, you are emphasizing the importance you place on creating a fair, respectful and discrimination-free work environment.

In writing your EEO policy, be aware that the law does allow you to exclude a certain protected group if you can prove that the exclusion is based on a "bona fide occupational qualification (BFOQ)." For example, if your organization runs a residential shelter for battered women, you may be able to exclude men from the position of live-in coordinator.

If you have questions about this, or other hiring issues, it's a good idea to speak with an employment attorney to identify your options in each particular situation.

Affirmative Action

Author's Comments

All employers are responsible for ensuring equal employment opportunity in their organizations, and for abiding by state and federal civil rights laws.

Whether or not you adopt a formal affirmative action policy depends on the size of your organization and the terms of any contracts you may have with governmental organizations.

An affirmative action plan is generally much more detailed than an EEO policy, and includes specific actions and strategies for recruiting, developing, promoting and retaining a diverse workforce. AA plans are usually developed and reviewed by an employment attorney. Any affirmative action plan must be backed up by the internal capacity and resources to implement it consistently. Your organization can be held accountable for non-compliance even if what you do or don't do is not, strictly speaking, illegal.

Creative Agency

(not applicable: no requirement)

By the Book Agency

(not applicable: no requirement)

Leading Edge Agency

In support of our commitment to equal opportunity in all matters relating to employment without regard to race, color, religion, disability, sex, veteran status, marital status, age or national origin we maintain a positive, continuing program of affirmative action.

We strive to achieve and maintain a diverse workforce. Toward that end, we undertake the following actions, which represent some but not all of our affirmative action efforts:

1. Fair and consistent hiring, promotion and salary administration practices that comply with our equal opportunity policy.

2. Communication about our equal employment opportunity policy to all employees on a regular basis.

3. Training for all supervisory employees on ways to support and develop a diverse workforce.

4. Regular reports to the Board of Directors on all activities and procedures designed to implement our policy of equal employment opportunity.

5. Implementation of focused recruitment strategies, if our staff does not meet our diversity goals.

Americans with Disabilities Act (ADA)

Creative Agency

(not applicable: size)

By the Book Agency

(see policy outlined below)

Leading Edge Agency

LEA welcomes applications from people with disabilities. We fully support the Americans with Disabilities Act (ADA) of 1990. We have taken steps to make our work facilities barrier-free and accessible as defined by state and federal statutes.

We have sought to identify the essential functions and physical requirements of all distinct jobs at LEA, and will make reasonable adjustments, through scheduling, task reassignment and other methods, to accommodate applicants and employees with disabilities.

Author's Comments

If you have 15 or more employees, you are required to comply with the ADA. Having a written ADA policy is a good first step, but ADA compliance requires that you put into practice specific procedures to ensure that you are not placing unnecessary barriers to employment before individuals with disabilities.

To fully comply with the ADA, an employer must identify the essential functions of each distinct job in the organization and be prepared to offer reasonable accommodations to allow a disabled applicant or employee access to the job.

The workplace must also be physically accessible, or the employer must be willing to make reasonable accommodations to the workplace (not to the extent of creating a financial hardship for the employer) to allow a person with disabilities to function in the job.

Handbook Use and Purpose

Creative Agency

The purpose of this staff member handbook is to outline certain information about your employment with Creative Agency. The policies described here are in effect and supersede all other versions of these policies previously given to you either orally or in writing.

The provisions of these policies may, at the discretion of our Board of Directors, be modified, revoked or changed from time to time. It also should be noted that our policies do not cover every situation that might arise in the workplace. Above all, we ask that you exercise common courtesy and common sense while on the job.

If you have questions regarding your employment or anything contained in these policies, please speak with your manager or our executive director.

By the Book Agency **BBA**

By the Book Agency's personnel policies were developed to facilitate consistent and equitable employment and personnel practices for all employees of the agency. This employee handbook is designed to assist employees in familiarizing themselves with important information about the agency, as well as information regarding their own privileges and responsibilities.

It is not possible to anticipate every situation that may arise in the workplace or to provide information that answers every possible question. Also, future circumstances may require changes in the policies, practices and benefits described in this handbook. Accordingly, the agency reserves the right to modify, rescind, supplement or revise any provision in this handbook. The agency will make reasonable efforts to provide employees with advance notice of any modifications or revisions to the handbook and will distribute updated pages as revisions are made.

It is important to note that this handbook only highlights the agency's policies, practices and benefits, and is not intended to be a legal document or contract. The policies and procedures in this handbook are intended to replace all previous personnel policies, practices and guidelines with the exception of the agency's at-will employment policy.

Any questions regarding the contents of this handbook may be addressed to your supervisor or to the director of administration.

Handbook Use and Purpose, continued

Leading Edge Agency

Welcome to Leading Edge Agency. This handbook outlines the policies and practices that guide us in our daily work together. We'd like you to know what you can expect from us, and what we will expect from you.

This handbook was created to serve three primary purposes: to present our policies and practices in one reference source; to conform to certain state and federal laws and convey necessary legal information to our employees; and to give a general description of Leading Edge's benefits. Nothing contained in this handbook should be perceived as stating or implying a contract of employment.

Underlying what we are communicating in this handbook is Leading Edge's desire to support individual performance and development and to provide the information necessary for all of us to make good decisions as we go about our daily work.

Please read this entire handbook and sign the acknowledgment at the back within your first two days of employment. You are responsible for knowing the contents of the handbook and using it as a guide. Of course, you may ask questions about our policies and procedures. Please speak with your supervisor or any member of the human resources staff at any time.

Please keep this handbook. We will notify you from time to time about changes in our policies and practices. The policies, procedures, benefits and practices described in this handbook should not be taken for granted and are subject to change. While we will attempt to give you ample notice when a policy or benefit change is made, there are circumstances under which advance notice will not be possible.

Underlying what we are communicating in this handbook is Leading Edge's desire to support individual performance and development and to provide the information necessary for all of us to make good decisions as we go about our daily work.

Work Eligibility

Author's Comments

All employers, regardless of size, are required to verify an employee's eligibility to be legally employed in the United States. This must be done within three working days of the employee's start date. Make certain that your new-hire practices include a procedure for viewing and photocopying all appropriate employee documentation and completing INS Form I-90. (Although photocopies of documents are not required by law, they are a practical way of providing proof of your compliance with IRCA.)

Be certain, however, not to keep copies of documents or I-90 forms in personnel files – these could be interpreted later as being used as the basis for discrimination. Remember, it is illegal to discriminate in employment on the basis of citizenship or national origin.

Creative Agency

Typically, on the first day at work all new staff members will be asked to fill out appropriate forms for payroll purposes and for personnel records. In accordance with the Immigration Reform and Control Act of 1986 (IRCA), all new staff members at Creative Agency are also required as a condition of employment to provide documentation that establishes their identity and legal right to work in the United States.

By the Book Agency

BBA

By the Book Agency seeks to comply with the requirements of federal law and employs only United States citizens and noncitizens who are lawfully authorized to work in the United States. All employment is conditioned on receipt, by the hiring supervisor or director of administration, of documentation establishing identity and authorization to work in the United States.

Leading Edge Agency

Our policy is to employ only those persons legally entitled to work in the United States without regard to citizenship, ethnic background or place of national origin. To conform with the Immigration Reform and Control Act of 1986 (IRCA), we hire only those who are eligible to work in the United States. We have adopted the following policies and procedures to encourage compliance with federal regulations and to facilitate our commitment to equal employment opportunity:

1. Except as required by law, no job applicant may be asked about, or categorized according to, citizenship or resident status. Hiring decisions will be made without considering such questions.

2. Applicants offered jobs will be told that they are required to produce satisfactory legal evidence of eligibility to work in the United States — such proof will be a condition of employment.

3. All new employees will be asked to provide actual documents verifying their eligibility to work legally in the United States and to complete an INS Form I-90 within three working days.

Introductory Period

Creative Agency

Your first 90 calendar days as a staff member are an introductory period. Certain benefits will not be available to you until the completion of this period.

During your introductory period, your manager will observe, and talk with you about, your job performance. This period also provides you with the opportunity to judge how well your new position suits you.

Your employment is a mutual relationship between you and Creative Agency, which either party may end during or after your introductory period. Completion of your introductory period is not a guarantee of continued employment.

By the Book Agency

BBA

Employees are considered introductory during the first one hundred eighty (180) days following the date of hire. During this period, performance will be carefully evaluated and a determination made regarding the employee's ability to perform. The fact that an employee has completed the introductory period does not guarantee continued employment. During the introductory period, employees are not eligible to take vacation or paid sick time.

Your employment is a mutual relationship between you and By the Book Agency, which either party may end during or after your introductory period.

Leading Edge Agency

LEA

The introductory period for all employees is meant to provide you and LEA with an opportunity to evaluate the working relationship. All employees will complete a minimum 90-day introductory period, and this period may be extended beyond 90 days upon review by your manager. The introductory period begins with your orientation, which includes a handbook review, and a review of your job description and short-term performance objectives. The remainder of your introductory period is spent increasing your familiarity with LEA and adjusting your skills to your specific job. After 30 days, and at the end of 90 days, you will participate in an evaluation process with your manager. However, feel free to discuss your job description and the contents of this handbook with your manager at any time.

Completion of your introductory period is not a guarantee of continued employment. Your employment is a mutual relationship between you and LEA, which either party may end during or after your introductory period without cause or advance notice.

Author's Comments

While it is very useful to establish an introductory period as a way of initiating a preliminary performance evaluation and for determining when an employee may begin to accrue and/or use benefits, don't mistake this as an "anything-goes" period. You are obligated to follow all state and federal employment laws from the minute an employee begins her/his first day on the job.

You may want to state here or in your disciplinary policy that any infraction of policy or serious performance problem can be grounds for dismissal during the introductory period – a kind of one strike and you're out policy. Further, it's important to convey that no employee is entitled to complete the full introductory period if job performance doesn't support continued employment.

Author's Comments

Many nonprofit managers find it difficult to distinguish between an exempt and a nonexempt employee. In determining which of your positions are which, you must follow the guidelines and exemption tests established by the Fair Labor Standards Act (FLSA) and California state law. The FLSA guidelines are available through the local office of the Employment Development Department. (The Management Center also offers nonprofits a one-page Help Sheet on exempt vs. nonexempt status.) In particular, I've found that many employers are not aware of the guidelines governing exempt employee pay. Do not allow exempt employees to take paid time off in half-day or hourly increments. If an exempt employee shows up to work for just one hour, s/he must be paid for a full day of work. Beginning in January 1998, nonexempt employees will receive overtime pay for hours worked in excess of 40 per workweek, but not for more than eight hours in one day.

Employee Classifications

Creative Agency

We place staff members into classifications based on job description, consistent with the Fair Labor Standards Act and applicable state law.

Exempt Employee — an executive, administrative or professional employee who is exempt from the provisions of the FLSA, usually paid an annual salary.

Nonexempt Employee — an employee (generally paid by the hour) who is eligible for overtime pay according to the provisions of the FLSA.

Regular Full-Time Employee — a salaried or hourly employee who is normally scheduled to work 35 hours or more per workweek and whose employment has no specified end date.

Regular Part-Time Employee — a salaried or hourly employee who is normally scheduled to work between 15 and 34 hours per workweek and whose employment has no specified end date.

Temporary Employee — an employee who is hired on a full- or part-time basis for a specified period of time, usually not to exceed six months.

On-Call Employee — a nonexempt employee who is not required to work a specified number of hours in any given workweek, but who is scheduled to work on an as-needed basis.

Inactive Employee — an employee who is on a leave of absence and is not receiving pay from Creative Agency.

By the Book Agency

(see policy outlined above)

Employee Classifications, continued

Leading Edge Agency

Your LEA employee classification is based on your job description and on the nature of the position, consistent with the Fair Labor Standards Act and all applicable California laws. Your classification determines how you are paid, whether you receive overtime pay and to what benefits you are entitled.

All employees are classified as either **exempt** or **nonexempt**, based on their position and the type of work they perform.

Exempt employees hold executive, administrative, professional or other exempt positions. Exempt employees are generally paid on a salaried basis, and their salary is intended to constitute their entire compensation, regardless of the number of hours they work.

Nonexempt employees perform work that does not meet the qualifications for exemption as defined by the FLSA. Nonexempt employees are generally paid by the hour and are entitled to paid breaks and overtime pay for working over 40 hours in one week.

Introductory employees are still working within their introductory period and are not eligible for most benefits until they have satisfactorily completed this period.

Full-time employees are those who are assigned a regular work schedule for 37.5 hours or more per workweek and whose assignment is indefinite (does not have a specified end date). Full-time employees are eligible for all employee benefits.

Part-time employees are those who are assigned a regular work schedule of less than 37.5 hours per workweek and whose assignment is indefinite (does not have a specified end date). Part-time employees are eligible for limited employee benefits, excluding medical, dental and vision coverage.

Temporary full-time or **part-time** employees are those who are assigned to work for a specified and limited period of time, usually less than six months. Temporary employees are eligible for legally mandated benefits such as Worker's Compensation Insurance and California State Disability Insurance.

Leading Edge Agency employs consultants and independent contractors from time to time. These individuals are not considered employees and are therefore ineligible for employee benefits, regardless of the length of the employment relationship.

> Your classification determines how you are paid, whether you receive overtime pay and to what benefits you are entitled. All employees are classified as either exempt or nonexempt, based on their position and the type of work they perform.

Changes in Employee Classification

Creative Agency

(not applicable: size)

By the Book Agency

(not applicable: size)

Leading Edge Agency

Your employee classification (which determines eligibility for benefits and/or overtime pay) may change over the course of your employment with LEA. If at any time you have a question about a possible change in your classification, please speak with your manager or our director of human resources.

Changes in your employee classification may be the result of a job change, a promotion or a change in either your work hours or your job description. Normally, a temporary change in job duties or work hours (for a period of up to four months) will not impact your employee classification.

Hiring of Relatives

Creative Agency

We have no prohibition against hiring relatives of our staff members. However, one general restriction has been established to help assure fair treatment of all staff members. While we will accept and consider applications for employment from relatives, family members will not be hired, promoted or transferred into positions in which they directly or indirectly supervise or are supervised by another family member.

Author's Comments

Having this policy is like carrying an umbrella so that it won't rain: It's those agencies without such a policy that end up wishing they had created one.

By the Book Agency

BBA

To foster an environment in which integrity and objectivity can be maintained, the By the Book Agency does not permit the employment of members of the same family in the same department.

For purposes of this policy, the term "family" applies to the following relationships, whether they are based on blood, marriage or other definitions: parent-child, sibling, grandparent-grandchild, aunt/uncle-niece/nephew, stepmother/father-stepchild, cousin, or spouse-spouse or spousal equivalent.

By the Book Agency does not permit an employee to work under the immediate supervision of a member of the same family. If such situations now exist, or if they develop in the future because of promotion, marriage, transfer or any other reason, the management of By the Book Agency reserves the right to transfer or terminate either or both employees, if necessary.

Leading Edge Agency

It is our policy to avoid bringing family relationships into the workplace whenever possible. However, on occasion, more than one family member may work for LEA. The following guidelines will govern those situations:

1. No employee will be permitted to hire a relative.

2. When related persons work for LEA, one relative may not supervise another.

3. Related persons will not be involved in evaluating each other's job performance or in making recommendations for salary adjustments, promotions or other budget decisions.

For the purposes of this policy, the term "family member" includes individuals related by marriage, blood or adoption, or by virtue of a domestic partnership.

The term "family member" includes individuals related by marriage, blood or adoption, or by virtue of a domestic partnership.

Position Descriptions

Author's Comments

Second only to the gruesome task of writing a personnel handbook is the creation of job descriptions. I encourage all nonprofits to take the time to develop and keep current job descriptions for each distinct position in the organization.

Job descriptions have many uses. In order to comply with the ADA, it is necessary to identify the essential functions of each job. Job descriptions are the basis of the hiring process and should be the foundation of a performance evaluation.

Don't think of a job description as a list of tasks or activities. Job descriptions should highlight the essential functions and the primary outcomes of the job. Job descriptions should answer the question "Why does this job exist?" not "What does this person do all day?" Be sure not to build the job description around an individual – it describes the job, not the person who does it.

Creative Agency

You will receive a position description outlining the primary functions and responsibilities of your job. Your position description is not designed to spell out all the duties and tasks associated with your employment; all our staff members are expected to fulfill both essential and secondary job duties and requirements. Position descriptions are not set in stone and will change, in whole or in part, over time. You are expected to discuss any significant changes in your functions and responsibilities with your manager, who has the authority to formalize changes in position descriptions at his or her discretion.

By the Book Agency

By the Book Agency strives to maintain a written job description for all positions. In the event that new paid positions are created through expansion or reorganization, written job descriptions will be prepared and then approved by the executive director before the position is filled.

A job description generally contains the following elements: title, summary of job duties, performance requirements, definition of essential and nonessential functions, qualifications (such as education or experience), title of the immediate supervisor, employee's signature, executive director's signature and date. Employees occasionally may be required to perform related duties not set forth in the job description. Job descriptions must be rewritten if the employee must undertake substantially new job responsibilities.

Leading Edge Agency

You will have received a position description as part of your orientation process. Read it carefully, and direct any questions you may have to your manager.

Position descriptions serve three purposes at LEA. First, they give prospective employees a clear understanding of the nature of an open position and facilitate the recruitment process. Second, they serve as a guideline for employees already working in established positions. Third, they assist LEA in complying with the Americans with Disabilities Act, by identifying the essential functions and physical requirements of each of our positions.

Position descriptions are dynamic documents, meant to be updated and revised continuously, based on the programs and services we offer. Generally, position descriptions are reviewed and revised as part of our annual performance appraisal process. We encourage you to offer suggestions on improving your effectiveness and the design of your position by speaking with your manager or our director of human resources.

Job Postings

Creative Agency

We post all full-time and part-time job openings internally via staff memo or daily announcements. The job may be posted and/or advertised externally at the same time, as appropriate. Jobs are internally posted for a minimum of five business days, and no job will be filled until the minimum posting period has ended.

By the Book Agency

BBA

It is the policy of the By the Book Agency to find the most qualified candidates to fill position vacancies. This will be accomplished through a combination of internal and external recruiting. Consideration will be given to the advancement of current employees, and employees are encouraged to apply for promotions or transfers for which they feel they are qualified.

Open positions may be posted for seven calendar days on bulletin boards at the discretion of the director of administration and/or the executive director. It is solely determined by By the Book Agency whether to fill positions from within or to hire from outside.

Only the director of administration and the executive director have the authority to extend job offers. All offers of employment will be in writing.

Leading Edge Agency

Our employment policy at LEA is to select the most qualified person available for a position based on knowledge, skills, experience and ability to perform job requirements. We are dedicated to internal promotion. We post all open positions internally, usually before any external posting or advertising begins. No hiring decision is made before all qualified internal applicants have been interviewed. In case we must choose between equally qualified candidates, we will give internal applicants preferential consideration.

Currently open positions are posted on specially designated bulletin boards. Descriptions of any position in the organization are available from our Human Resources Department. If you are interested in an open position, you may request a confidential, exploratory meeting with a member of our Human Resources staff before deciding to apply. Once you are an official candidate, you are required to tell your current manager of your interest in the other position, as s/he may be asked to give the hiring manager a reference regarding your current job performance.

Author's Comments

Many employees are concerned about losing an opportunity for advancement to an outside hire. Carefully think through your own philosophy on internal transfers and promotions, and craft a policy that you can live with. Few policies are scrutinized more by employees than those concerning job postings.

Transfers and Promotions

All Agencies

To be eligible to apply for a transfer or promotion, an employee must have been in his/her current position for at least six months and must be meeting the requirements of the current position. Employees on a written warning dealing with job performance or unacceptable behavior are ineligible for transfers or promotions. Any exceptions to these policies must be approved by the executive director.

Performance Evaluations

Creative Agency

In addition to your 90-day performance review at the completion of your introductory period, you also will participate with your manager in an annual performance review process. As part of this process, you and your manager will assess your accomplishments during the previous year, and set new performance goals for the coming year.

By the Book Agency

BBA

Each employee's performance will be reviewed on a continual basis by his/her immediate supervisor. A formal year-end performance appraisal will be conducted coinciding with the agency's fiscal year-end. While the mechanics of the performance appraisal process may change from time to time, any process will include these components: planning, goal setting, measurement, communication and feedback.

Annual performance appraisals, with both the employee's and supervisor's signatures, are placed in the employee's personnel file. Employees may keep a copy of their appraisal, and also have the opportunity to comment on it in writing. The performance appraisal also includes a discussion about career planning and development.

Author's Comments

If you are a small agency you may not need to have a formal policy about transfers and promotions. In larger organizations, it's a good idea to determine how long an employee must be in one job before applying for another. Larger organizations also find it helpful to specify that employees on written warning are not eligible for transfers (to avoid transferring a problem from one department to another).

Performance Evaluations, continued

Leading Edge Agency

(LEA)

The annual performance evaluation process at LEA is an opportunity for a regular and periodic review of your job performance. During the evaluation process, you and your manager will assess your performance in relation to objectives you have previously agreed upon and identify areas of strength as well as areas needing development. In addition, you and your supervisor will develop goals and objectives for the next review period, and identify the ways in which your supervisor will support your further development.

LEA's annual performance evaluation process, which takes place at the close of our fiscal year, is based on the following principles:

- Performance goal setting and evaluation are two-way processes involving both employee and supervisor

- Employee performance is evaluated on objective, job-related criteria that have been communicated to you in advance

Setting goals and objectives for future performance is as important as evaluating past performance. The objectives of LEA's performance evaluation process are:

1. To let our employees know how they are doing on the job

2. To encourage communication and two-way feedback on the expectations and goals of both employees and the agency

3. To provide a fair and consistent method for making pay decisions

4. To document performance in ways that will assist future supervisors and facilitate transfers, promotions and improvement plans

5. To be a tool for coaching, planning and professional development

At LEA, we believe that it is important for our employees to know exactly how well they are doing in relation to our established standards of performance.

Author's Comments

Although not required by law, performance evaluations are an important tool for clarifying performance standards, encouraging skill development and emphasizing key organizational values. Performance evaluations are an essential component of any pay-for-performance system.

Setting goals and objectives for future performance is as important as evaluating past performance.

Employee Referral Bonus Program

Author's Comments

I'm a fan of referral bonus programs for employees. In today's labor market it is increasingly difficult to attract qualified applicants, especially for entry-level positions. A referral bonus program provides an incentive for your employees to act as contingency recruiters – and who knows your organization better than they?

Creative Agency

(not applicable: size)

By the Book Agency

(see policy outlined below)

Leading Edge Agency

LEA's Referral Bonus Program encourages staff members to refer qualified external applicants for employment. Any current LEA employee who refers a successful candidate for an open position will receive a paid day off, to be used within three months of the referral's first day on the job.

Speak with our human resources director for more information about the program. Members of the Human Resources staff, the executive director and the direct hiring manager for a given opening are not eligible to participate in the Referral Bonus Program.

Employment of Board Members

Author's Comments

Based on my own experience as a member of several nonprofit boards, I believe it's very important to develop and follow a strict policy about the hiring of board members.

All Agencies

In order to preserve the objectivity and integrity of the agency's Board of Directors, any member who wishes to apply for employment with the agency must first resign from the board.

Health Insurance

Creative Agency

At Creative Agency we believe our staff members should have access to health insurance coverage for themselves and their dependents. We strive to provide all our staff members with adequate health care benefits and work in partnership with our health care providers to ensure access for all our staff members.

Full-time staff members and their dependents are eligible for medical and dental coverage through our HMO. Creative Agency pays 100 percent of the premiums for all full-time staff, and we pay 25 percent of the premiums for eligible dependents.

Part-time staff members are eligible to apply for medical coverage through an alternate health care provider; the cost of premiums for our part-time staff members and their dependents is borne entirely by them.

As with most policies, our benefits coverage is subject to change. For more information about health care coverage, please speak with our office manager.

By the Book Agency

BBA

MEDICAL INSURANCE

Eligible full-time employees may choose from two medical coverage options. The cost of medical insurance is shared by the employee and By the Book Agency. Coverage begins on the first day of the month following completion of the introductory period. Coverage ends on the last day of the month in which the employee is employed.

DENTAL INSURANCE

Dental insurance is available on a shared-cost basis. Coverage begins on the first day of the month following completion of the introductory period. Coverage ends on the last day of the month in which the employee is employed.

As with most policies, benefits coverage is subject to change. Please speak to the office manager if you have questions about medical or dental insurance.

Author's Comments

There are almost as many health plan options in California as there are nonprofits, and a discussion about choosing among them is beyond the scope of this handbook.

You should choose employee health insurance benefits and cost-sharing options specifically tailored to the needs and resources of your organization. The three examples provided here are designed to give you an idea of how health insurance benefits can vary from one organization to another.

The Management Center's annual *Wage & Benefit Survey* contains detailed information about the types of benefits offered by nonprofits of all sizes throughout Northern California.

Health Insurance, continued

If an employee has medical coverage from another source, such as a spouse's medical plan, the employee may apply the monthly amount LEA nornally would spend on the medical insurance premium to a wellness account.

Leading Edge Agency

HEALTH AND WELLNESS

LEA establishes a health and wellness account for each of our full-time employees. After completing 30 days of employment, each full-time employee receives a monthly health and wellness deposit equal to health coverage costs for the employee through one of the three health care plans LEA offers.

Upon completion of six months of satisfactory continuous employment, our full-time employees with eligible dependents receive an additional monthly deposit equal to 50 percent of the cost of dependent coverage (through the same health care plan).

WELLNESS OPTION

If an employee has medical coverage from another source, such as a spouse's medical plan, the employee may apply the monthly amount LEA normally would spend on the medical insurance premium to a wellness account. Proof of health insurance coverage from an outside source is required for participation in the wellness account.

An employee participating in the Wellness Option may use the monthly income in one of two ways:

1. Place it in the LEA 401(3b) savings plan
2. Apply it to the cost of a monthly health club membership

Definitions, for Eligibility

CREATIVE AGENCY

For the purposes of benefits coverage, Creative Agency defines "immediate family" as a spouse or domestic partner, child (including stepchild and foster child), parents and siblings.

For the purposes of benefits coverage, we define "domestic partnership" as an eligible staff member and one other person sharing a committed relationship that includes: living together, financial interdependence, joint responsibility for each other's common welfare and each considering the other to be a life partner.

Please note: The definitions noted above pertain only to specific benefits; eligibility for these benefits is described on the following pages.

By the Book Agency

BBA

For the purposes of benefits coverage, "immediate family" is defined as spouse or partner, parent, parent-in-law, sibling, child, grandchild or grandparent.

Leading Edge Agency

LEA

Certain benefits, such as health insurance coverage, family care leave and bereavement leave, use the term "immediate family" or "domestic partner" in descriptions of eligibility and/or coverage. At LEA we define "immediate family" as your spouse or domestic partner, children (including stepchildren and foster children), siblings (including stepsiblings and siblings-in-law), parents (including step-parents and parents-in-law) grandparents or grandchildren.

At LEA we recognize domestic partners as spousal equivalents, providing that both the employee and domestic partner satisfy the following requirements:

- Are 18 or older
- Are unmarried
- Are not related to each other
- Share an intimate, committed relationship of mutual caring of at least six months' duration
- Live together
- Agree to be responsible for each other's basic living expenses
- Currently do not have a different domestic partner
- Execute a Declaration of Domestic Partnership Affidavit

Author's Comments

Everyone's definition of "immediate family" might differ, so it's best to formally define yours for the purposes of benefits eligibility – in the case of bereavement leave, for example, or for sick time to be used to care for a member of the family.

Even if you do not offer health insurance coverage to domestic partners, it is helpful to define the term for other benefits, such as bereavement leave, Family Care Leave or use of sick time.

Insurance Continuation

Author's Comments

A handbook is not the place to spell out all the details and guidelines for insurance continuation (COBRA). The handbook should inform employees of their basic right to continuation; more detailed information should be provided at the time of eligibility.

Employers with 20 or more employees are required to offer insurance continuation under COBRA. You may check with your insurance carrier about your options for voluntarily offering insurance continuation.

Because COBRA regulations require employers to follow complex procedures and to adhere to strict timelines, COBRA administration should be assigned to a qualified administrator or manager in your organization.

Creative Agency

The Consolidated Omnibus Budget Reconciliation Act of 1986 (COBRA) guarantees continuous coverage of health and dental insurance to eligible employees and their dependents (at the employee's expense) at group rates that otherwise might have been forfeited when employment ends.

At the time of the creation of this manual, Creative Agency did not qualify for COBRA coverage because of our size. If this status changes, we will notify all staff members.

Our health insurance carrier does offer a conversion coverage plan to all staff members at the time of termination of employment. If you are covered by our health insurance and leave our employ, the carrier will notify you of the option and cost of continuous coverage.

By the Book Agency

BBA

Upon termination, employees covered under a health insurance plan have certain legal rights to remain on the insurance plan at their own expense for up to 18 months (more in some exceptional cases) through COBRA benefits. More information regarding COBRA coverage, costs and administrative procedures is available from the Finance Department at the time employment ends or when an employee has a question about other qualifying events.

Leading Edge Agency

(see policy outlined above)

Workers' Compensation

Creative Agency

Our staff members are protected by workers' compensation insurance for all illness or injury arising from and occurring within the scope of their employment.

If you are injured on the job, notify your manager immediately, no matter how minor the injury may seem.

It is our policy to return an injured staff member to work as soon as possible on modified or light-duty status until the time that a physician's release to return to regular work is obtained.

By the Book Agency

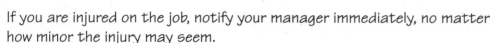

BBA carries workers' compensation insurance coverage as required by law to protect employees who are injured on the job. This insurance provides medical, surgical and hospital treatment in addition to compensation for loss of pay resulting from work-related injuries or illness. The cost of this coverage is paid by BBA.

You must immediately report any on-the-job injury to your supervisor, regardless of how minor the injury may be. Questions concerning our workers' compensation coverage should be directed to the office manager.

BBA does not provide workers' compensation coverage for injuries sustained during or as a result of an employee's voluntary participation in off-duty social, recreational or athletic activities that are not part of an employee's work-related duties. When an employee is required or expected to participate in a recreational, social or athletic activity as part of his or her job, then workers' compensation coverage may apply.

Leading Edge Agency

All employees are protected by our workers' compensation insurance policy while employed at LEA. The policy is available at no cost to you and covers cases of injury or illness resulting from legitimate work activities. By law, we are required to report injuries covered under workers' compensation within 24 hours. Please immediately report any on-the-job injury to your manager or a member of the Human Resources staff.

Complete information about workers' compensation and on-the-job injuries is available from our Human Resources Department.

Author's Comments

Workers' compensation is legally mandated for all employers in the state of California. In addition to the basic information in your handbook, you should train all employees in the basics of preventing and responding to on-the-job injuries. Most workers' compensation insurance carriers provide safety training and educational information to client organizations. Ask about your carrier's training and education programs.

Disability Insurance

Author's Comments

Employees are often confused about the differences in benefits offered by workers' compensation insurance, group medical insurance and California State Disability Insurance. Designate someone in your organization as the benefits expert, and make sure that all your employees know they can speak with that person to get answers to their health insurance questions.

Creative Agency

Each of our staff members contributes to California State Disability Insurance. Contributions are made through payroll deductions. California State Disability Insurance is payable when you cannot work because of illness or injury not related to employment, when you are disabled due to pregnancy or when you are entitled to workers' compensation at a rate that is less than your daily disability benefit amount.

Coverage begins on your first day of employment and ends on your last. For more information about California State Disability Insurance, please speak with our office manager.

By the Book Agency

BBA

Employees of BBA who become disabled due to illness or injury (including pregnancy) may receive state-funded income protection insurance for the time they are unable to work. The determination of benefits is up to the state of California. An employee may apply for disability benefits after being disabled for eight days, or if hospitalized, after one day of disability. Forms can be obtained from the director of operations, the local office of the California Employment Development Department or the employee's physician.

If a physician deems an employee to be temporarily disabled, he or she cannot return to work without first submitting a medical release to his or her supervisor.

Leading Edge Agency

SHORT-TERM DISABILITY (STD)
(see the California State Disability Insurance policies outlined above)

LONG-TERM DISABILITY INSURANCE (LTD)
LEA provides LTD coverage at the agency's expense to insure that you receive a percentage of your salary if you must miss work due to a disability. You are eligible for LTD coverage following a 90-day introductory period. LTD benefits begin after 90 days of continuous, doctor-certified disability. Your benefit is equal to 60 percent of your predisability base pay. LTD benefits coordinate with other disability programs.

Please contact our Human Resources Department as soon as possible after a disabling event to receive more information about this coverage.

Life Insurance

Creative Agency

All regular full-time staff members are covered under our life insurance plan. The plan offers a benefit equal to your annual base salary or annualized hourly wage. You must delegate a beneficiary to whom this benefit will be paid in the event of your death. The full premium for this benefit is paid for by Creative Agency.

By the Book Agency

Regular full-time employees are eligible for a basic Life and Accidental Death and Dismemberment Insurance plan paid for by the agency. Employees may elect supplemental coverage as well as dependent life insurance coverage at their own expense. Coverage begins on the first day of the month after one full month of employment, and ends on the last day of the month in which employment ends.

Leading Edge Agency

(see policy outlined above)

Author's Comments

Life insurance coverage is a basic benefit that most employers can afford to offer. If your benefits budget won't allow you to pay the premiums, consider offering life insurance coverage at the employee's own expense.

Vacations

Creative Agency

We offer paid vacation time to eligible staff members for their rest and recreation away from work. Creative Agency recognizes the value of time away from work responsibilities and encourages staff members to use all accrued vacation benefits on a timely basis.

Because we believe that time away from work is beneficial for rest and rejuvenation, we do not allow staff members to take pay in lieu of vacation time.

ELIGIBILITY

All regular staff members who work an average of 35 hours per week or more begin to accrue vacation time on the first day of employment; however, staff members may not take time off for vacation until they complete six months of continuous service.

ACCRUAL

Regular full-time staff members earn paid vacation at their regular rate of pay, computed hourly, as follows:

Length of Service	Hours per Pay Period	Hours per Year
0 - 12 months	3.077	80
13 - 36 months	5	120
37 or more months	6.67	160

Regular part-time staff members (those who work 15 or more hours per week) earn paid vacation on a prorated basis, determined by the number of hours they are regularly scheduled to work per week.

MAXIMUM ACCRUAL

All eligible staff members are expected to use accrued vacation benefits each year. Regular full-time staff members cannot accrue more vacation than they earn in 12 months. Only after some accrued vacation time is used will new vacation time begin accruing again. Exceptions to this policy, based on extraordinary circumstances, require the approval of the staff member's manager and the executive director.

SCHEDULING

Accrued vacation may be taken after completion of the first six months of employment. Vacation requests must be made at least 30 days in advance and require the approval of the executive director. Conflicting requests will be decided by length of service.

Author's Comments

Most employers now mandate some type of limit – or "cap" – on vacation accruals, to prevent employees from building up huge reserves of paid vacation. Not only are large amounts of paid vacation time difficult to schedule, but it can be hard on an employer's budget to pay out large amounts of accrued vacation when an employee leaves. Caps also are useful in preventing burnout in employees who can never find the time to take a vacation (especially when they know they can keep accruing it indefinitely).

California law prohibits employers from having a "use it or lose it" policy; you cannot take away vacation time once it has been accrued. You can cap accruals at a certain level and require accrued vacation to be used before additional time begins accruing. Although vacation pay is not a legally required benefit, all employers should encourage employees to plan for and take regular vacations as one way of balancing work and personal life.

Vacations, continued

By the Book Agency

BBA

Regular full-time employees earn paid vacation time on the following schedule, beginning with the first day of employment:

1 - 3 years: 12 days each calendar year (90 hours)

4 - 10 years: 15 days each calendar year (120 hours)

11+ years: 20 days each calendar year (150 hours)

Regular part-time employees scheduled to work 20 or more hours per week earn paid vacation time on a prorated basis based on the number of hours worked per week.

No other classification of employee earns paid vacation time.

At the end of each calendar year employees may carry over accrued, unused vacation pay. However, employees must take accrued and carried-over vacation by April 1 of the following year in order to continue to accrue additional vacation time.

In extraordinary circumstances when vacation cannot be taken in the approved time frame, the executive director may grant approval to carry over time beyond the allotted period, while regular accrual continues.

All vacation time must be requested and approved in advance. Employees with five or more years of service may take vacation time for the current year in advance of its being accrued.

Employees may not receive pay in lieu of vacation. When they leave the organization, employees will be paid for any accrued, unused vacation.

> At the end of each calendar year employees may carry over accrued, unused vacation pay. However, employees must take accrued and carried-over vacation by April 1 of the following year in order to continue to accrue additional vacation time.

Vacations, continued

You begin to earn

vacation time

on your first day

of employment,

but you must

complete six months

of employment

before using

accrued vacation.

Leading Edge Agency

We encourage employees to take vacations to refresh themselves and to ensure the high quality of their work.

FULL-TIME EMPLOYEES

As a full-time employee you earn up to 15 paid vacation days each year. Paid vacation time is accrued on a monthly basis at the rate of 1.25 vacation days per month. You begin to earn vacation time on your first day of employment, but you must complete six months of employment before using accrued vacation.

PART-TIME EMPLOYEES

As a part-time employee you earn paid vacation days on a prorated basis each year, based on the standard of 15 days for 2,080 hours of work annually. You begin to earn vacation time on your first day of employment, but you must complete six months of employment before using accrued vacation.

ACCRUAL MAXIMUM

Vacation time can accrue to a maximum of 20 days. Once this cap is reached, no further vacation time will accrue until some vacation is used. There is no retroactive grant of vacation time for the period of time the accrued vacation compensation was at the cap. Any exceptions to this policy require the written approval of our executive director.

ADDITIONAL VACATION

Employees who have completed five years of service accrue an additonal day of vacation for each year of employment, to a maximum of 30 days of annual vacation. For example, if you have completed five years of employment, you accrue 20 days of vacation annually (15 days plus an additional five).

SCHEDULING

You are expected to exercise consideration and good judgment when requesting vacation days from your manager. If you request vacation during a particularly busy time, or at a time when many others have also requested time off, you may be required to postpone your vacation. Generally, we ask that you request vacation time at least 30 days in advance.

Holidays

Creative Agency

All regular staff members receive paid time off for the following holidays:

- New Year's Day
- Martin Luther King Jr. Day
- Presidents' Day
- Memorial Day
- Independence Day

- Labor Day
- Thanksgiving Day
- The Friday after Thanksgiving
- Christmas Eve Day
- Christmas Day

Regular part-time staff members receive holiday pay on a prorated basis.

By the Book Agency

BBA

The holiday schedule is published by the executive director at the beginning of our fiscal year. By the Book Agency observes the following holidays:

- New Year's Day
- Martin Luther King Jr. Day
- Presidents' Day
- Memorial Day
- Independence Day

- Labor Day
- Thanksgiving Day
- The Friday after Thanksgiving
- Christmas Eve Day
- Christmas Day

All regular full-time employees are paid eight hours' wages for each holiday. Regular part-time employees are paid for holidays on a prorated basis, determined by the number of hours worked in a workweek. Part-time employees who do not work on the day on which a holiday falls may observe the holiday on a different day of the week by arranging for this in advance with their supervisor.

Any nonexempt employees required to work on a holiday will be paid at time and a half their regular rate of pay for hours worked that day and will be granted paid time off on another day equivalent to the number of hours worked on the holiday. This alternative paid time off must be taken within one month of the holiday worked.

Any exempt employees required to work on a holiday will be paid at time and a half their regular rate of pay for that day and will be granted an alternative paid day off, to be taken within one month of the holiday worked.

Temporary employees do not receive holiday pay.

Employees on vacation at the time a holiday occurs will not have that day counted as vacation pay.

Author's Comments

If you have a diverse workforce, it is a good idea to build some flexibility into your paid holiday benefit by offering personal days or optional paid holidays.

On a practical note, identifying in advance when you will observe holidays that fall on weekends assists your employees in planning family time, etc.

You are not legally required to offer paid holidays. The following three examples show typical holidays offered by nonprofits, but you may choose to offer different paid holidays, based on your organization's needs.

Holidays, continued

We offer our employees paid holidays throughout the year to facilitate participation in national holidays and to provide opportunities for celebration of religious and ethnic holidays.

Leading Edge Agency

We offer our employees paid holidays throughout the year to facilitate participation in national holidays and to provide opportunities for celebration of religious and ethnic holidays.

The following are official holidays for all LEA employees — these are days on which our offices will be closed:

- New Year's Day
- Martin Luther King Jr.'s Birthday
- Memorial Day
- Independence Day
- Labor Day
- Thanksgiving Day
- Day after Thanksgiving
- Christmas Day

Full- and part-time employees who regularly work at least 20 hours per week receive holiday pay for the days listed above. Temporary employees and part-time employees who work less than 20 hours per week take these days off without pay.

Eligible part-time employees who do not work on the day on which a holiday falls may observe the holiday on a different day of the week by arranging for this in advance with their supervisor.

When a holiday falls on a Saturday, the office will be closed on the preceding Friday to observe the holiday. When a holiday falls on a Sunday, the office will be closed on the following Monday to observe the holiday.

All eligible employees also may choose two additional holidays from the following list for a total of 10 paid holidays per year.

Optional holidays are:

- Employee's birthday
- Anniversary
- Christmas Eve Day
- Kwanzaa
- Valentine's Day
- Chinese New Year
- Fiesta San Jacinto
- St. Patrick's Day
- Good Friday
- Emancipation Day
- Cinco de Mayo
- Yom Kippur
- Rosh Hashanah
- Fiestas Patrias
- Dia de los Muertos

Floating Personal Days

Creative Agency

Personal days are for use at your discretion for personal business or to allow you to observe additional religious or ethnic holidays. Personal days cannot be combined with vacation time.

Regular full-time staff members earn one paid personal day for every six months worked. Personal days are accrued as of your hire date initially, and thereafter on January 1 and July 1 of every calendar year.

Regular part-time staff members earn one paid personal day per calendar year of service.

Personal days cannot be carried over from year to year; if you do not use them, you lose them. You are not paid for accrued, unused personal days when your employment at Creative Agency ends.

By the Book Agency

BBA

FLOATING HOLIDAYS

In addition to paid holidays, two floating holidays are provided each year to regular full-time employees, to be used for special occasions such as birthdays or ethnic or religious holidays. Regular full-time employees earn two floating holidays in their first year if they are employed before July 1; after July 1, one floating holiday in their first year. In succeeding years, employees are granted two floating holidays per year.

Regular part-time employees who are scheduled to work 20 hours or more per week are eligible for floating days at the rate of one-half of the full-time rate.

Temporary or part-time employees working less than 20 hours per week do not receive floating holidays.

Floating holidays must be used in the calendar year in which they are granted. When they leave the organization, employees will be paid for floating days not used.

Leading Edge Agency

(see policy for Personal Use Time, page 40)

Author's Comments

Whether you call them personal days, floating holidays or floating personal days, it's a good idea to offer employees flexible paid days off to accommodate personal responsibilities, religious holidays and family obligations.

Author's Comments

I encourage employers to allow employees to use paid sick leave for caring for a sick child as well as for those times when they themselves are ill. Your employees with children will greatly appreciate the gesture, and you will not be putting otherwise ethical individuals in the position of having to lie about an absence.

Sick Time

Creative Agency

We provide paid sick time to regular full- and part-time staff members to provide you with protection against loss of income if you are ill or injured, or if you need time off from work for necessary or routine health care.

ACCRUAL

Regular full-time staff members earn sick time at the rate of eight hours per month of work.

Regular part-time staff members earn sick time on a prorated basis, determined by the number of hours worked per week.

Staff members may accrue up to a maximum of 24 days of sick time. Upon reaching the maximum, no further sick time will be accrued until some of the accrued time has been used.

USE

Staff members who are ill or injured and anticipate being away from work for more than one week should speak with their health care provider or our office manager for information about State Disability Income benefits.

Under some circumstances, we may require verification of a staff member's medical condition, especially if a pattern of frequently used sick time develops.

PAYMENT

We do not offer pay in lieu of use of accrued sick time, and staff members do not receive payment for accrued sick time when they leave our employ.

Sick Time, continued

By the Book Agency   BBA

Sick time provides regular full- and part-time employees with paid time off to recover from illness or injury. Sick time may also be used by regular part-time employees for health care appointments that cannot be scheduled outside work hours.

ACCRUAL AND PAYMENT

Regular full-time employees accrue sick time at the rate of one day per month of service for a total of 12 days per year. Regular part-time employees accrue sick time on a prorated basis, based on the number of hours they regularly work per month.

Sick time may be carried over from one year to the next, but accrual caps at 60 days until some sick time is used.

Sick time is accrued from the start of employment, but cannot be used until the employee satisfactorily completes the introductory period.

No payment is made for accrued, unused sick time upon separation.

SICK TIME USE

Employees are responsible for directly notifying their supervisor when prevented from starting or continuing a workday due to illness or injury. Employees must also keep their supervisor informed about the expected duration of the time away from work.

In most circumstances, a doctor's statement is required when an employee uses more than five consecutive days of sick time, or when an accumulation of absences seems to establish (in the supervisor's judgment) a problematic use of sick time. By the Book Agency may request verification of the reasons for any use of sick time.

Employees may use sick time to care for ill family members, but the same verification requirements apply in these instances.

Employees are responsible for directly notifying their supervisor when prevented from starting or continuing a workday due to illness or injury. Employees must also keep their supervisor informed about the expected duration of the time away from work.

Leading Edge Agency

(See Personal Use Time, next page)

Personal Use Time

Author's Comments

Many employers are choosing to provide their employees with flexible paid time off instead of sick time, to be used for illness, a mental health day or personal business that cannot be taken care of outside work hours.

It is best to analyze your employees' use of paid sick time, personal days and vacation time, and to understand the budget consequences before choosing to offer flexible paid time off.

Creative Agency
(not common practice)

By the Book Agency
(not common practice)

Leading Edge Agency

We recognize that we all have responsibilities outside of work. Additionally, we want to offer our employees some protection against loss of income due to personal or family illness. Therefore, in lieu of sick time, LEA provides regular employees with Personal Use Time off from work to be used for any of the following:

- Personal illness or injury
- Family illness or injury
- Appointments — routine or otherwise — that cannot be made outside work hours
- Wellness
- Observance of personal, religious or ethnic holidays not covered by alternative holiday pay

ACCRUAL

All regular staff members who have successfully completed the introductory period will be granted Personal Use Time at the beginning of each fiscal year (prorated based on hire date for the first year of employment):

- Regular full-time: 15 days per year
- Regular part-time: 7 days per year

At the end of each fiscal year, you may donate any unused Personal Use Time to the Time Share Bank (see page 41); otherwise, you must forfeit it.

USE
- Exempt employees may take Personal Use Time in increments of one day.
- Nonexempt employees may take Personal Use Time in hourly increments.

We expect all employees to use paid time off responsibly. Employees are asked to schedule Personal Use time in advance whenever possible. It may be necessary, from time to time, for a manager to request documentation of a personal or family illness. Any employee believed to be abusing paid time off or establishing a pattern of absence that disrupts our services will be subject to disciplinary action up to and including termination. Personal Use Time cannot be combined with vacation pay except with the advance approval of our human resources director.

Employees do not receive payment for accrued, unused Personal Use Time when they leave LEA, nor do we offer employees pay in lieu of use while they are with LEA.

Time Share Bank

Creative Agency
(*not common practice*)

By the Book Agency
(not common practice)

Leading Edge Agency

(LEA)

At LEA we all care about the welfare of our fellow employees. To provide a channel for goodwill and good wishes, we created the Time Share Bank.

The Time Share Bank enables any employee to donate accrued Personal Use Time to colleagues who are experiencing a medical emergency or catastrophic illness that requires substantial time off from work. Any regular employee may donate Personal Use Time, in increments of eight hours, to the Time Share Bank at any time during the year. Forms for this purpose are available from our Finance Department.

Those who, due to a medical emergency or catastrophic illness, have used up all their available paid time off and need additional income to supplement California State Disability Income, can apply for a grant from the Time Share Bank. Time is granted in eight-hour increments.

The amount of funds available in the Time Share Bank at any given point is determined by the total salary dollars represented by the time donated, not by the actual number of hours donated.

APPLYING FOR TIME SHARE BANK HOURS

Employees may apply for Time Share Bank hours through their manager or a member of the Human Resources staff. To qualify for a grant, an employee must have exhausted all of his or her available paid time off.

Grants are made on a first-come, first-served basis and are given based on the following criteria:

1. Employees must have regular status and have completed six months of employment.

2. The amount of time in the bank and the number of applicants.

3. Employees may not have received a previous grant within the past 12-month period.

TAX CONSEQUENCES

There are no tax consequences to an employee who donates accrued time to the Time Share Bank; the donating employee may not claim the leave as income or as a deductible expense or loss. The employee receiving the donated time, however, does have tax consequences, in that paid time off received by the employee will be considered as income for employment tax purposes.

Flexible Spending Account

All Agencies

All regular full- and part-time staff members may choose to enroll in our Flexible Spending Account program, which allows staff members to set aside pretax dollars to be used for uninsured medical expenses (such as your out-of-pocket amount or vision care) and/or dependent care services.

Essentially, this benefit allows you to stretch your income a bit by using tax-free dollars to pay for medical expenses not covered by insurance and for child care and other eligible dependent care expenses.

PROCEDURE

- Eligible staff members may enroll in the program upon hire or at the start of a new plan year. The plan year normally runs from June 1 to May 31. Enrollment forms are available from our office manager.

- Money is automatically taken out of each paycheck; no taxes are withheld from this amount.

- Staff members submit receipts for reimbursement to our office manager; reimbursements are made on a monthly basis for health care expenses and on a biweekly basis for dependent care.

A WORD OF CAUTION

No refunds of money left in an individual's spending account are given at the end of the plan year. This means that staff members participating in the plan need to estimate expenses carefully. Money remaining in all staff members' FSAs at the end of the plan year is pooled and divided equally among the accounts of continuing participants who also participated in the plan during the previous year.

Please see our office manager for more information regarding Flexible Spending Accounts.

Education and Professional Development

Creative Agency
(not applicable: size)

By the Book Agency

By the Book Agency supports employees who wish to enhance their professional development and job-related skills through external education programs and conferences. In addition, employees may be asked to attend conferences and training forums as participants or presenters. Employees must have the prior approval of their supervisor to attend outside development events.

BBA covers the costs of outside training and conferences based on organizational benefit and annual budget. All agency-covered trainings and conferences require the approval of the executive director and are subject to change based on budgetary constraints.

Leading Edge Agency

In addition to on-the-job learning and training, LEA encourages employees to enhance professional development and job-related skills through external education programs and conferences. Up to five paid days per calendar year are provided for regular full-time employees who wish to enhance job-related skills by, for example, attending external training programs and seminars. Educational leave does not carry over from year to year. Time off (whether paid or unpaid) for external training and continuing education requires advance approval by the employee's supervisor.

Employees may be asked to attend conferences, workshops and educational meetings on behalf of the agency. In these instances, LEA will cover most travel, lodging, registration and meal expenses. Employees will receive regular pay while attending required outside conferences. Days spent attending required educational/professional development events will not be deducted from annual educational leave.

While we do not cover the cost of continuing education for our employees, we will attempt to accommodate continuing education through flexible scheduling for those employees who are attending school while working.

Author's Comments

If you pay for outside training and education, it is very important to create clear guidelines about who is eligible and how to initiate the approval process. You want to encourage employees to develop themselves professionally, but you do not want to create inequities in the way such a policy is put into practice by inadvertently favoring one class, or education level, over another.

Employee Assistance Program

Author's Comments

An increasing number of organizations are providing an Employee Assistance Program (EAP) as an employee benefit. EAPs provide counseling services and advice to employees with drug or alcohol problems, marital troubles, financial problems, child care concerns or other personal problems that can have a negative impact on their productivity and morale. Numerous local and national companies provide this benefit for employees, usually through confidential telephone counseling. Your health insurance broker can often provide information about the costs and types of EAPs available in your area.

Creative Agency

(not applicable: size)

By the Book Agency

(not applicable: size)

Leading Edge Agency

There may be occasions when an employee's work performance is jeopardized by unresolved personal problems. Examples of this include financial crisis, family difficulties, drug or alcohol abuse and gambling. LEA's policy is to make it possible for the individual employee to get the help s/he needs and to restore her/his job effectiveness.

We will make available, on a confidential basis through our Human Resources Department, the phone number of a professional, confidential counseling service, the services of which are paid for by LEA. No employee's job security or promotional opportunity will be jeopardized because he or she has sought and conscientiously followed a program of treatment.

Voluntary acceptance of a treatment program is not a valid reason for continued poor job performance. Poor job performance resulting from apparent behavior or personal problems is handled in the same manner as any other substandard performance.

Reporting to work under the influence of drugs or alcohol, or possessing drugs or alcohol on our property, will result in immediate termination.

Employees who suspect they have a problem are urged to take advantage of our Employee Assistance Program and to voluntarily follow through with any recommended treatment.

Elder Care

Creative Agency
(*not common practice*)

By the Book Agency
(not common practice)

Leading Edge Agency

If you have the regular responsibility of providing care for an elderly relative, we encourage you to take advantage of our flexible scheduling arrangements. You may use accrued Personal Use Time to care for an elderly parent or relative.

Through our Flexible Spending Account program you may be able to set aside tax-free dollars to use for expenses associated with the care of an elderly dependent. Please see our Human Resources Department for more information.

If you anticipate needing significant or regular amounts of time off because of a parent's serious health condition, please consult the Leaves of Absence section, which details our Family and Medical Leave policy.

Author's Comments

An increasing number of employees are responsible for providing some care for an elderly parent. This type of benefit is greatly appreciated by employees who sometimes get left out of the picture when it comes to dependent care benefits.

If you have the regular responsibility of providing care for an elderly relative, we encourage you to take advantage of our flexible scheduling arrangements.

New Baby

Author's Comments

While your organization may not have the resources to offer a financial gift to new parents, you may offer time off, paid or unpaid, under the Family and Medical Leave Act or on a voluntary basis.

Creative Agency

(not common practice)

By the Book Agency

(not common practice)

Leading Edge Agency

Employees who are welcoming a newborn or newly adopted child receive a $100 treasury certificate for future financial assistance. The certificate is redeemable when the child reaches 18 years of age. Employees are responsible for filling out the "New Addition to My Family" form available from the Human Resources Department.

Credit Union

Creative Agency

(not applicable: size)

By the Book Agency

BBA

BBA has established an affiliation with the Northern California Credit Union. The credit union offers employees a range of savings, investment and loan options at favorable interest rates. Payroll deduction is available for those employees wishing to make regular monthly contributions. Information and forms may are available from the finance director.

Leading Edge Agency

(see policy outlined above)

Parking Space

Creative Agency
(not applicable: size)

By the Book Agency
(not applicable: size)

Leading Edge Agency

Our facilities have limited access to parking, and we encourage you to take public transportation to work whenever possible.

Each month one parking space at each of our facilities is designated for the Team Player of the Month. This designation is selected monthly by an anonymous vote of all regular staff at the facility. It goes to the one employee who gets the most votes that month for "teamwork above and beyond the call of duty."

Each year, our Board of Directors holds a luncheon honoring all those employees selected as Team Players of the Month.

Each month one parking space at each of our facilities is designated for the Team Player of the Month. This designation is selected monthly by an anonymous vote of all regular staff at the facility.

Disability Leave

Creative Agency

Eligibility: Full- and part-time staff members of Creative Agency are eligible for unpaid medical leave after they complete the introductory period (exceptions for pregnancy disability leave may apply). Medical leaves are granted when a staff member is temporarily unable to perform his or her job due to illness, injury, pregnancy and/or childbirth. Medical leaves are granted for the duration of the disability, up to a maximum of six months.

Requesting a Leave: If you become disabled, you should promptly notify your manager. Written certification from your physician or other licensed health practitioner stating the nature of your disability, the date your disability began and the expected date of your return to work should be provided to your manager. We may request that you provide us with additional medical verification of your continuing disability from time to time during the course of your leave as well.

Pay During Leave: Staff members must use any accrued sick leave at the beginning of a medical leave. After accrued sick leave is used up, a staff member may use accrued vacation time or apply for California State Disability benefits or Workers' Compensation insurance benefits, whichever is appropriate. Staff members are considered inactive when they are no longer being paid and are on a medical leave.

Return to Work: Staff members returning from leaves resulting from pregnancy, childbirth or other related medical conditions will be guaranteed re-employment in the same position except when, due to organizational necessity, a position has ceased to exist during the leave. In that event, we will seek to provide the returning staff member with a substantially similar position.

Staff members returning from other types of medical leave will be returned to the same or a similar position whenever possible; however, Creative Agency cannot guarantee re-employment.

You may be asked to provide a physician's certification of your fitness to return to work. Your manager should be told of any change in the date of your return to work in advance.

Disability Leave, continued

End of Employment: A staff member away from work on a medical leave will be considered to have voluntarily resigned from Creative Agency if:

- The staff member fails to notify the agency of her availability for work after the disability ceases
- The staff member fails to return to work after the disability has ceased and a position is available

A staff member who resigns because she has exceeded the maximum leave time allowed will be given special rehire consideration when she is able to return to work.

Maximum leave time does not apply in cases of work-related illness or injury.

Benefits During a Medical Leave: Creative Agency will continue to provide insurance benefits to staff members during a medical leave, provided that the staff member regularly continues to pay her share of the premium, if applicable.

Benefits that accrue for hours worked will not accrue during a medical leave. Leave time will be counted toward seniority, however.

A staff member

who resigns because

she has exceeded

the maximum leave

time allowed will be

given special rehire

consideration

when she is able

to return to work.

Disability Leave, continued

Disability leave

is available to an

employee whose

physician certifies

that the employee

is temporarily

disabled from

performing his/her

job because of illness,

injury, physical or

mental impairment,

pregnancy and/or

childbirth.

By the Book Agency   BBA

MEDICAL DISABILITY LEAVE

Disability leave is available to an employee whose physician certifies that the employee is temporarily disabled from performing his/her job because of illness, injury, physical or mental impairment, pregnancy and/or childbirth. After using accrued sick time, an employee may elect to use accrued vacation, provided that the employee gives advance notice of this election to the supervisor prior to or at the time of commencement of the leave. If accrued vacation is to be used, it shall be used at the beginning of the leave or immediately after any accrued sick time is exhausted. Following the use of accrued sick and vacation time, the remainder of the leave shall be unpaid. Employees on disability leave should apply promptly for State Disability Insurance, Workers' Compensation Insurance, and/or long-term disability benefits, whichever is applicable.

Medical certification of disability must be submitted at or before the start of a disability leave of absence and at least every 30 days of leave thereafter, stating the nature of your disability and the expected date of return to work. Requests to extend an initial leave must be accompanied by supporting medical certification and must be received by the supervisor at least two working days in advance of the previously estimated return date. An employee returning to work from a disability leave must give at least two days' advance notice to the supervisor and, upon returning to work, must submit a written release from the employee's physician.

PREGNANCY AND/OR CHILDBIRTH LEAVE

A pregnancy and/or childbirth leave is not to exceed four months in any 12-month period and does not have to be continuous. Employees returning from a pregnancy and/or childbirth leave of absence of four or fewer months will be returned to their same job unless, for organizational reasons, BBA was unable to hold the job open or to fill it temporarily because to do so would have resulted in an undue hardship on BBA. Under these circumstances, BBA will offer the employee a substantially similar job if one exists that the employee is qualified to perform.

WORK-RELATED ILLNESS OR INJURY LEAVE

A leave of absence due to a disabling work-related illness or injury is generally not limited in duration. Employees returning from such a leave will be returned to their same job unless, for organizational reasons, BBA was unable to hold the job open or to fill it temporarily because to do so would have resulted in an undue hardship on BBA. Under these circumstances, BBA will offer the employee a substantially similar job if one exists that the employee is qualified to perform.

Disability Leave, continued

NON WORK-RELATED ILLNESS OR INJURY LEAVE

A leave of absence necessitated by a disabling, nonwork-related illness, injury or medical condition that is temporary or of relatively short duration may not exceed two months in any 12-month period and does not have to be continuous. Employees returning from such a leave of two months or fewer will be returned to their same job unless, for organizational reasons, BBA was unable to hold the job open or to fill it temporarily because to do so would have resulted in an undue hardship on BBA. Under these circumstances, BBA will offer the employee a substantially similar job if one exists that the employee is qualified to perform.

BENEFITS DURING A MEDICAL LEAVE

BBA will continue to pay for insurance coverage for employees during the unpaid portion of a medical leave up to a maximum of four months. Beyond this time, if additional leave is approved, employees participating in health insurance coverage will be given the option of paying for continued coverage for the duration of the leave.

Benefits that accrue for hours worked will not accrue during a medical leave. Leave time will be counted toward seniority, however.

RESIGNATION DURING A MEDICAL LEAVE

Failure either to comply with BBA's certification and notice requirements during a leave or to return from a leave on the first working day following the end of the leave will be considered a resignation on the part of the employee.

Employees returning from a leave of two months or fewer will be returned to their same job unless, for organizational reasons, BBA was unable to hold the job open or to fill it temporarily because to do so would have resulted in an undue hardship on BBA.

Author's Comments

Consider using the following question-and-answer format to spell out your policy regarding Disability Leave or Family and Medical Leave (see next page). This format can help employees grasp the many details required of such a policy, or to locate the answer to a specific question about one aspect of your policy.

We require that

you use any accrued,

unused Personal

Use Time at the

beginning of your

Disability Leave.

You then may choose

to use accrued,

unused Vacation

Time or to begin

an unpaid leave.

Disability Leave, continued

(LEA)

Leading Edge Agency

WHO IS ELIGIBLE FOR DISABILITY LEAVE?
An LEA employee who is temporarily disabled due to illness, injury, pregnancy or childbirth may be eligible for an unpaid leave of absence for a period equal to the duration of the disability, up to a maximum of six months in a 12-month period. If you are temporarily disabled due to a work-related illness or injury, your leave will extend for the duration of your disability or until your disability is determined to be permanent, whichever comes first. Additional information about work-related disability leaves is available from the Human Resources Department.

HOW DO I APPLY FOR DISABILITY LEAVE?
If you become disabled, you should promptly notify your manager. Written certification from your doctor or other licensed health practitioner stating the nature of your disability, the date your disability began and the expected date of your return to work should be provided to your manager. We may request that you provide us with additional medical verification of your continuing disability from time to time during the course of your leave.

CAN I USE ACCRUED PAID TIME OFF DURING A DISABLITY LEAVE?
We require that you use any accrued, unused Personal Use Time at the beginning of your Disability Leave. You then may choose to use accrued, unused Vacation Time or to begin an unpaid leave. You may be eligible to receive State Disability Insurance benefits, which are administered by the California Employment Development Department. Information is available through the CEDD and our Human Resources Department.

HOW DOES A DISABILITY LEAVE AFFECT MY JOB?
Employees returning from leaves resulting from pregnancy, childbirth or other related medical conditions are guaranteed re-employment unless, for organizational reasons, LEA was unable to hold the job open or to fill it temporarily because to do so would have resulted in an undue hardship on LEA. If this occurs, LEA will offer the employee a substantially similar job if one exists that the employee is qualified to perform. Employees returning from other types of disability leave will be returned to the same or a similar position whenever possible; however, LEA cannot guarantee re-employment.

CAN I RESIGN WHILE ON DISABILITY LEAVE?
A staff member away from work on a medical leave will be considered to have voluntarily resigned from LEA if s/he gives notice of resignation in writing while on the leave, if s/he fails to notify the agency of her/his availability for work after the disability ceases or if s/he fails to return to work after the disability has ceased and a position is available. An employee who resigns because s/he has exceeded the maximum leave time allowed will be given special rehire consideration when s/he is able to return to work. Maximum leave time does not apply in cases of work-related illness or injury.

CAN I COMBINE FAMILY AND MEDICAL LEAVE WITH DISABILITY LEAVE?
An employee may take a maximum of seven months (four months of Disability Leave plus 12 workweeks) of combined Disability and Family and Medical Leave only when she is actually disabled by her pregnancy for four full months and then immediately takes 12 workweeks of baby-bonding family leave.

Family and Medical Leave

Leading Edge Agency

An unpaid leave of absence for family or medical care will be granted to all eligible employees for up to 12 weeks in a 12-month period. The 12-month period is measured beginning with the month in which the requested leave starts.

WHO CAN TAKE FAMILY AND MEDICAL LEAVE?
An employee is eligible for leave after s/he has worked for LEA for more than 12 months, and for at least 1,250 hours during the 12-month period immediately prior to the date the leave begins.

WHAT IS FAMILY AND MEDICAL LEAVE?
Family and Medical Leave is an unpaid leave of up to 12 workweeks in a 12-month period. The leave is for the birth and care of an employee's newborn child; the placement with the employee of a child for adoption or foster care; the serious health condition of an employee or an employee's spouse, domestic partner, child or parent.

WHAT RESTRICTIONS APPLY TO THE WAY LEAVE IS TAKEN?
Leave may be taken intermittently — in two or more blocks of time — or by reducing the employee's normal weekly or daily work schedule. Employees should try to schedule leave in a way that minimizes disruption to our organization's operations.

HOW WILL TAKING FAMILY AND MEDICAL LEAVE AFFECT MY JOB?
Employees who take Family and Medical Leave will return to the same or a comparable position.

WHAT EFFECT WILL FAMILY AND MEDICAL LEAVE HAVE ON MY BENEFITS?
LEA will maintain existing benefits coverage during the leave period. Employees are required to continue co-payments (when applicable) during the leave.

A Family and Medical Leave will not be considered working time for the purposes of accrual of vacation and health and wellness leave.

CAN I USE ACCRUED PAID TIME OFF DURING THIS LEAVE?
Employees are required to apply any accrued paid time off (vacation, health and wellness) toward Family and Medical Leave.

HOW MUCH NOTICE DO I NEED TO GIVE BEFORE TAKING FAMILY AND MEDICAL LEAVE?
Employees are required to provide 30-day advance notice of the need to take leave when the need is foreseeable and such notice is possible. Thirty days prior to taking the leave or, if less, as soon as the need for a leave is known, employees should inform both their manager and the human resources director of their intention to take the leave.

CAN FAMILY AND MEDICAL LEAVE BE DENIED?
In certain circumstances, an employee may be denied a leave if it will cause substantial and grievous economic injury to LEA.

Family and Medical Leave is an unpaid leave of up to 12 workweeks in a 12-month period... Leave may be taken intermittently — in two or more blocks of time — or by reducing the employee's normal weekly or daily work schedule.

School Leave

Creative Agency

(not applicable: size)

Employees who take school-related leave must make arrangements for the time off with their supervisor as soon as the need for the leave is known.

By the Book Agency

BBA

An employee who is the parent, guardian or custodial grandparent of a school-age child may take up to 40 hours of leave per school year for the purpose of participating in the child's school activities or to discuss the child's possible suspension. In taking such leave, employees may take unpaid time off or use accrued vacation time. School-related leaves cannot exceed eight hours in any calendar month.

Employees who take school-related leave must make arrangements for the time off with their supervisor as soon as the need for the leave is known. By the Book Agency may request written documentation from the school reflecting the date and time of the activity attended.

No discriminatory action will be taken against any employee because he or she takes school-related time off.

Leading Edge Agency

LEA

We encourage our employees with school-age children to be involved with their children's education. To facilitate school involvement, we provide all employees with up to 16 hours of paid time off per year to participate in school-related activities or to meet with teachers and/or school administrators.

In addition to paid time off, employees may take an additional 24 hours of unpaid leave for school-related activities during the school year. Employees may apply accrued personal time to school-related time off. We do ask that you take no more than eight hours per month of school-related time off.

Employees must make arrangements for taking school-related time off with their manager as far in advance as is practical. Your manager may request that you provide documentation of a particular school activity or event.

Drug or Alcohol Rehabilitation Leave

Creative Agency

(not applicable: size)

By the Book Agency   BBA

By the Book Agency recognizes that drug and alcohol abuse are serious medical problems and wants to assist employees who realize that they have such a problem, which may interfere with their ability to perform their job in a satisfactory manner. Employees who decide to enroll voluntarily in a rehabilitation program due to a problem with drugs or alcohol use will be given time off to participate in such a program, and By the Book Agency will make reasonable efforts to keep this fact confidential.

In order to be granted a leave for this purpose, the employee must submit certification of enrollment in a drug/alcohol rehabilitation program at or before the leave begins. The certification must include a statement that the employee's participation in the program prevents him/her from working, and must specify beginning and ending dates of the program and the employee's estimated date of return to work. An extension of the leave requires supporting documentation prior to the end of the initial leave.

Employees returning from such a leave will be returned to their same job unless, for organizational reasons, BBA was unable to hold the job open or to fill it temporarily because to do so would have resulted in an undue hardship on BBA. Under these circumstances, BBA will offer the employee a substantially similar job if one exists that the employee is qualified to perform.

Leading Edge Agency

(see policy outlined above)

Author's Comments

California employers of 25 or more employees must reasonably accommodate an employee who wants to participate in an alcohol or drug rehabilitation program. However, this law does not protect an employee whose job performance is hampered significantly by drug or alcohol use from disciplinary action or termination.

Long-Term Illness or Permanent Injury

Employees will be returned to their same job, unless, for organizational reasons, the agency was unable to hold the job open or to fill it temporarily because to do so would have resulted in an undue hardship on the agency.

All Agencies

An employee whose leave is necessitated by a disabling, nonwork-related physical or mental impairment, which substantially limits one of the employee's major life activities and is expected to be ongoing for a substantial period of time or is of permanent duration, may be accommodated with longer and more frequent leaves as long as such leaves will not result in an undue hardship on the agency.

Such employees will be returned to their same job, unless, for organizational reasons, the agency was unable to hold the job open or to fill it temporarily because to do so would have resulted in an undue hardship on the agency. Under these circumstances, the agency will offer the employee a substantially similar job if one exists that the employee is qualified to perform.

Jury and Witness Duty

Creative Agency

Both exempt and nonexempt staff members are eligible for up to one week's paid leave when called upon to serve as a juror or witness at a trial. You will be asked to provide documentation showing your required days of attendance. If you are released by the court after serving a partial day, you are expected to report to work and complete your normal workday unless you make other arrangements with your manager.

Exempt staff members who are required to serve longer than a week, and who do some work for Creative Agency during each of the remaining weeks served, will continue to receive full pay while on jury duty.

By the Book Agency **BBA**

Regular full-time and regular part-time employees who are called to serve on a jury will be granted up to two weeks' paid leave, and will be granted unpaid leave for the remainder of their jury duty. Temporary employees will be granted an unpaid leave for the period of their service. Employees may keep any compensation received in exchange for their jury duty.

Exempt employees who are required to serve longer than two full weeks, and who do some work for BBA during each of the remaining weeks that they serve, will continue to receive full pay while on jury duty.

Proper documentation demonstrating the required time away from work may be requested prior to granting the leave. If an employee is not required to report, or is released early from jury or witness duty, the employee must immediately report to work.

All employees will be granted an unpaid leave if called to serve as a witness in a legal proceeding.

Author's Comments

While you are not required by law to pay employees for jury or witness duty, you must grant them leave to serve. Most nonprofits offer some paid leave – enough to cover the typical length of jury duty service. Since courts generally pay a stipend to jurors, you can choose to deduct this amount from jury duty pay.

Jury and Witness Duty, continued

We will grant regular employees up to 20 days of paid jury duty or witness leave in a calendar year. Court-mandated time beyond 20 days will be unpaid.

Leading Edge Agency

If you receive a proposed juror questionnaire, or are called as a witness in a legal proceeding, please notify your manager as soon as possible. If you are called as a juror during a particularly busy time, we may ask you to request the court to postpone your jury duty to a more convenient time.

We will grant regular employees up to 20 days of paid jury duty or witness leave in a calendar year. Court-mandated time beyond 20 days will be unpaid.

Please keep your manager informed of your jury duty or witness status. On days when you serve less than a full day at court, contact your manager to determine whether or not you should return to work. When you return from serving as a juror or witness, you may be required to furnish your manager or our human resources director with appropriate documentation.

Exempt staff members who are required to serve longer than 20 days, and who do some work for LEA during each of the remaining weeks that they serve, will continue to receive full pay while on jury duty.

Bereavement Leave

Creative Agency

Regular staff members receive up to three paid days per occurrence for bereavement leave in cases of a death in the immediate family. This leave allows time for making funeral arrangements and attending the funeral. Staff members who need additional time to attend to the affairs of the deceased or for personal reasons may request to use accrued vacation or sick time, or to take time off without pay.

By the Book Agency

Regular full- and part-time employees will be granted up to three days of leave, paid at the employee's daily rate of pay, determined by the number of hours the employee is regularly scheduled to work per week, in the event of a death in the employee's immediate family.

Leading Edge Agency

Bereavement leave of up to five days with pay is provided to regular full and part-time employees in the event of a death in the immediate family. You may also seek time off for bereavement leave in the event of the death of a significant person in your life, even if the person is not an immediate family member. We will be as flexible as possible in accommodating these leave requests. Employees seeking paid time off for bereavement leave should communicate with their manager about leave arrangements.

If the cost of a plane ticket would otherwise prevent an employee from attending the funeral of a member of his or her immediate family, LEA provides limited financial assistance in the form of a no-interest loan for air travel.

Regular staff members receive up to three paid days per occurrence for bereavement leave in cases of a death in the immediate family.

You may seek time off for bereavement leave in the event of the death of a significant person in your life, even if the person is not an immediate family member.

Military Leave

Author's Comments

Federal law requires employers to treat reservists and members of the National Guard who are deployed into active service, and employees who are drafted into service, as you would any other employee on a protected leave. This means that you must reinstate them to the same or a similar position with the same seniority, benefits and pay as when they left.

Employers are not required to continue to pay an employee on military leave.

Creative Agency

We seek to comply with all state and federal laws regarding leaves of absence for military duty. Please speak with your office manager or the executive director in the event that you need to schedule such a leave.

By the Book Agency

Employees who are or who become members of the National Guard or Reserves will be granted a leave of absence to attend military training in either mandatory or voluntary status, for a maximum period of 15 calendar days annually. BBA will cover the difference between an employee's regular pay for the period and the pay received by the military when training is mandatory. Such pay will not be provided to cover lost earnings in the case of voluntary training.

Employees who leave BBA employment for active duty; active duty for training; initial active duty for training; inactive duty training; full-time National Guard duty; or examinations to determine fitness for duty in any branch of the armed forces of the United States will be reinstated with accrued tenure (including seniority and accrued benefits) in accordance with the provisions of the Uniformed Services Employment and Re-employment Rights Act of 1994.

Employees must advise their supervisors of their military training schedule as far in advance as possible.

Leading Edge Agency

If you are a member of the National Guard or Reserves and are directed to participate in periodic field training, you will receive unpaid military leave for a maximum period of 15 calendar days a year. Such leave will have no impact on your regular vacation accrual. If you have some choice as to when to attend yearly training, we ask that you select a period that will be convenient for the organization and for your co-workers.

Employees who are indefinitely deployed in active service via the draft or by order of the President of the United States are entitled to military leave. Such a military leave is without pay, and ends either 90 days after an employee's discharge from the service, or one year after the employee is released from hospitalization continuing after discharge. The employee will be reinstated to his or her former position or to a position of similar seniority, status and pay if the LEA is informed of the discharge no fewer than 60 days prior to the employee's planned return to work.

Personal Leave

Creative Agency

We have a policy of granting a personal leave of absence in exceptional cases when time away from work will allow a staff member to deal with an unexpected and serious personal situation. A personal leave of absence may be granted for up to a maximum of 30 workdays.

A personal leave will not be considered an interruption of service for benefits purposes; however, no benefits based on time worked will accrue during such a leave. If you feel you need a personal leave, you should discuss your circumstances with your manager.

If you do not return from a personal leave on or before the last day of the leave, you may be considered to have resigned from Creative Agency.

By the Book Agency

Employees are expected to maintain a continuous record of employment. However, we recognize that it may be necessary for an employee to be excused from work for personal reasons. In such cases, employees must submit a request for a personal leave of absence as far in advance as possible. All requests will be given every consideration consistent with the urgency and need of the employee's circumstances, the employee's job performance and the department's work load. Authorization for such personal leaves of absence is fully at the discretion of the executive director.

Personal leaves of absence are without pay and are available to full and part-time employees who have completed one year of service. Failing to return to work upon completion of the leave, or working for another employer during the leave without prior approval, will be considered a resignation.

A personal leave of absence of no more than 30 days will not be considered an interruption of continuous service with respect to benefit plans. Employees on personal leaves of more than 30 days may continue insurance coverage by paying the cost of the monthly premium. Benefits that normally accrue for hours worked will not accrue during a leave. Upon returning from a personal leave, an employee will have the same amount of seniority as he or she had when the leave began.

Author's Comments

While you are not required by law to provide any unpaid personal leave time, you are more likely to retain dedicated employees if you provide them with some flexibility to deal with life's unexpected crises and opportunities.

As with any leave policy, be sure you spell out who is eligible, what is the maximum length of the leave and whether or not you will provide benefits coverage during the leave.

Personal Leave, continued

All personal leaves are granted at the discretion of management, based on our needs related to your position and the hardship that might result from your absence at a particular time.

Leading Edge Agency

Occasionally, employees face compelling personal needs that may require them to take time off from work. LEA would prefer that an employee request a personal leave of absence rather than resign. This allows us the possibility of working through the situation rather than losing a valued resource.

To be eligible for a personal leave you must have completed at least one year of continuous employment and have received a satisfactory performance evaluation. All personal leaves are granted at the discretion of management, based on our needs related to your position and the hardship that might result from your absence at a particular time.

If granted, personal leaves cannot exceed 90 days. These leaves are unpaid, although LEA will continue to provide health benefits coverage for the duration of the leave. Employees on personal leave do not accumulate service time, but keep their existing seniority upon return to active status.

Failure to return to work immediately following the leave of absence is regarded as a voluntary resignation.

Sabbatical Leave

Creative Agency
(not common practice)

By the Book Agency
(not common practice)

Leading Edge Agency

In order to encourage employees to periodically step back from the day-to-day concerns and pressures of our work, we offer a six-week, unpaid sabbatical leave to all regular full- and part-time employees. To be eligible for sabbatical leave, employees must complete five years of continuous service and have a satisfactory job performance rating as evidenced by the two most recent evaluations at the time the leave is requested.

Sabbatical leaves require the approval of the executive director and must be arranged at least three months in advance. Employees returning from sabbatical leave will be reinstated to the same or a substantially similar position. While benefits do not accrue during sabbatical leave, LEA will continue to pay for health insurance coverage during the leave.

Eligible employees may apply for sabbatical leave once every five years.

To be eligible for sabbatical leave, employees must complete five years of continuous service and have a satisfactory job performance rating as evidenced by the two most recent evaluations at the time the leave is requested.

Time Off to Vote

Creative Agency

Nonexempt staff members may receive paid time off to vote in city, state or federal elections. Since polling places are generally open before and after work, we ask that you make every effort to vote outside of your normal working hours. Staff members unable to vote before or after work must make advance arrangements with their manager for reasonable time off to vote at the beginning or end of their normal work hours.

Exempt staff are not paid by the hour, and there will be no salary impact if an exempt staff member takes time to vote during the workday.

By the Book Agency

Employees who are unable to vote in an official public election during nonwork hours may arrange, with at least 48 hours' advance notice, to take up to two hours off from work, with pay, to vote. Advance approval for such time off must be obtained from the employee's supervisor.

Leading Edge Agency

(see policies outlined above)

Safety Policy

Creative Agency

Creative Agency expects its staff members to work in a safe manner, to use good judgment and common sense in matters of safety, to observe all safety rules published and posted in various areas and to follow all federal and state OSHA regulations. At the time of hire, all new staff members receive a safety orientation, including training on disaster preparedness.

If you have any questions or concerns about workplace safety, or if you would like to review our complete safety program, please speak with your office manager.

By the Book Agency

BBA

BBA strives to provide a safe and healthful workplace and to prevent accidental injury through employee training and education. BBA maintains a safety manual with complete information on all aspects of our safety program.

BBA managers and supervisors are responsible for overseeing the safety programs of the organization. All supervisors are required to see that every employee has read the BBA safety rules. Furthermore, supervisors are expected to enforce all safety rules as the strongest method of preventing accidents and injuries.

It is the responsibility of the director of operations to oversee proper care, storage and maintenance of all equipment and potentially hazardous materials (including chemicals such as toner or cleaning agents). The operations staff regularly conducts safety reviews of work areas and takes steps to correct any potentially hazardous situations.

All employees and volunteers are required to work in a safe and responsible manner. Safety requirements for employees and volunteers include:

- Considering safety as a daily on-the-job priority
- Following all safety rules and work procedures
- Immediately reporting any unsafe condition, accident or near miss to their supervisor
- Maintaining a clean and orderly work area
- Only working with equipment or materials with which they are familiar and for which they've been properly trained
- Always wearing seatbelts when traveling on agency business

Any willful violation of a safety procedure can result in immediate termination of employment.

Author's Comments

All employers, regardless of the size of their staff, should emphasize the importance of safety on the job. A handbook is a good place to state some general policies about workplace safety and health. This type of general policy statement does not fulfill the requirements for compliance with SB198, which requires all employers to prepare and implement an Illness and Injury Prevention Program, the details of which are beyond the scope of this handbook. The California Chamber of Commerce has many health and safety publications, including an SB198 Handbook, the contents of which are applicable to nonprofit employers.

Safety Policy, continued

Leading Edge Agency

LEA strives to provide each of our employees and volunteers with a safe, comfortable and healthy work environment.

We provide all employees with the tools, training, facilities and information necessary to work in a safe and efficient manner. We ask you to approach your work with a thoughtfulness that reflects your respect for your own health and safety and that of your fellow employees.

LEA strives to comply with all workplace safety laws and regulations — employees are responsible for taking the opportunities provided to understand them and observe them. Our fundamental belief is that no one task is so important that it warrants risking the health or safety of any employee at any time. Safety and emergency procedure information is available from the safety coordinator in your department or from your manager.

If you have any questions or concerns about workplace health or safety, please speak to your manager or any member of our Human Resources staff. If any employee at any time wishes to report an unsafe or hazardous workplace situation, s/he may do so anonymously by placing a call to our Safety Hotline at 956-SAFE.

We provide all employees with the tools, training, facilities and information necessary to work in a safe and efficient manner. We ask you to approach your work with a thoughtfulness that reflects your respect for your own health and safety and that of your fellow employees.

Drug-Free Workplace

Creative Agency

All staff members are expected to understand and comply with the following guidelines regarding the use of drugs or alcohol in the workplace:

1. We prohibit the unlawful use, possession, distribution, sale or manufacture of a controlled substance on our premises.

2. We prohibit all staff members from being under the influence of drugs or alcohol while on the job. Exceptions for medicines are made on a case-by-case basis.

3. Failure to follow CA's drug-free workplace policy may result in disciplinary action including suspension without pay, mandatory participation in a drug rehabilitation program on the first offense and termination on the second.

4. If you are convicted of violating any criminal drug statute in the workplace, you are required to notify the executive director within five calendar days of the conviction.

Author's Comments

California's Drug-Free Workplace Act of 1990 is almost identical to the federal act, but applies to persons or businesses contracting with or receiving grants from the state of California. The federal Drug-Free Workplace Act of 1988 applies to all employers who receive grants of any size from the federal government and to contractors who do $25,000 or more in business with the federal government. If you determine that you are required to follow the federal and/or state requirements for a drug-free workplace, you should consult with your labor attorney or review a labor law publication to learn what you need to do to be in compliance.

Many nonprofit employers choose to institute a strict anti-drug policy, even when they are not required by the terms of state or federal grants.

Drug-Free Workplace, continued

Any employee who reports to work while under the influence of drugs or alcohol runs the risk of endangering his or her safety, the safety of others, the destruction of (or damage to) personal or agency property and a loss of productivity and workplace morale.

By the Book Agency   **BBA**

As part of BBA's ongoing commitment to a safe and healthy workplace, this agency maintains a drug-free workplace policy. Any employee who reports to work while under the influence of drugs or alcohol runs the risk of endangering his or her safety, the safety of others, the destruction of (or damage to) personal or agency property and a loss of productivity and workplace morale.

All employees and volunteers of BBA are required to understand and comply with the agency's drug-free workplace policy. Any failure to comply with the guidelines of this policy can result in immediate termination of employment. Employees and volunteers either in BBA's offices or conducting business on behalf of BBA regardless of location are prohibited from:

- Unauthorized use, possession, purchase, sale, manufacture, distribution, transportation or dispensation of any controlled substance.

- Reporting to work while under the influence of alcohol or a controlled substance. Controlled substances include, but are not limited to:
  1. Narcotics (heroin, morphine, etc.)
  2. Cannabis (marijuana, hashish)
  3. Stimulants (cocaine, diet pills, etc.)
  4. Depressants (tranquilizers)
  5. Hallucinogens (PCP, LSD, "designer drugs," etc.)

- Use, possession, purchase, sale, manufacture, distribution, transportation or dispensation of any legal prescription drug in an illegal manner.

- Reporting to work while impaired by the use of a legal drug whenever such impairment might substantially interfere with job performance or pose a threat to the employee's safety or the safety of others, or risk significant damage to BBA property.

CONVICTION NOTIFICATION

An employee who is convicted of violating a criminal drug statute must inform the executive director or operations director of this agency (including pleas of guilty or nolo contendere) within five days of the conviction. Failure to so inform the agency will result in disciplinary action up to and including termination of employment.

Drug-Free Workplace, continued

SUBSTANCE ABUSE EDUCATION AND TREATMENT

BBA offers regular training to supervisors to assist in identifying and addressing substance abuse on the job. In addition, BBA periodically offers an education program for all employees on the dangers of substance abuse in the workplace.

For employees who seek help in overcoming drug and alcohol abuse problems, BBA offers the following rehabilitative assistance:

1. Medical benefits for substance abuse treatment
2. Information about community resources for treatment

An employee who voluntarily enters a substance abuse treatment program will not be penalized or discriminated against in any way by the agency.

Employees who violate the drug-free workplace policy may, at the discretion of management, be required to attend a rehabilitation or drug abuse assistance program as an alternative to disciplinary action. Employees given this opportunity must satisfactorily participate in the program as a condition of continued employment.

Leading Edge Agency

(see policies outlined above)

Employees who violate the drug-free workplace policy may, at the discretion of management, be required to attend a rehabilitation or drug abuse assistance program as an alternative to disciplinary action.

Smoking

Author's Comments

Most California employers must prohibit smoking in any enclosed area of the workplace. If you employ five or fewer people you may permit smoking in enclosed areas under certain limited conditions.

To prevent second-hand-smoke wars, it is helpful to designate places where employees may smoke if you have a large number of smokers and operate in your own separate facility.

Creative Agency

In consideration of the health and safety of all our staff members, we maintain a smoke-free environment.

By the Book Agency

Smoking is prohibited in all BBA offices.

Leading Edge Agency

Smoking is not permitted in any LEA facility. If you smoke, please demonstrate consideration for your fellow employees when you choose an outside smoking location.

LEA encourages those employees who smoke to quit. If you are interested in the smoking cessation program offered through our health maintenance organization, please contact our benefits administrator in Human Resources.

Use of Personal Fragrance

Author's Comments

A policy that addresses this issue is becoming increasingly popular as individuals with a sensitivity to fragrances are becoming more vocal.

Creative Agency
(not common practice)

By the Book Agency
(not common practice)

Leading Edge Agency

Some of our employees are highly sensitive to perfumes, colognes and other personal fragrances. We ask that you consider the sensitivities of others before you choose to wear fragrances at work. Any employee who is experiencing a problem with perfumes, etc. worn by a fellow employee is encouraged to respectfully request that the work area be kept fragrance-free.

Workweek

Creative Agency

Our workweeks are Sunday through Saturday.

By the Book Agency

The workweek commences at 12:01 a.m. Monday and ends at midnight Sunday. The standard workweek for a full-time employee is 37.5 hours.

Leading Edge Agency

(see policies outlined above)

Author's Comments

It is important to define your workweek if you have a large number of hourly, nonexempt employees, particularly if they work flexible schedules or weekends. This prevents confusion about the specific hours and/or days represented on a single paycheck.

Pay Periods

Creative Agency

We pay staff members twice a month. Payday is the 10th and the 25th of the month, unless that payday falls on a holiday or weekend. In that case, staff members will be paid on the last working day before the holiday or weekend.

By the Book Agency

For all employees, the standard pay period is semimonthly (15th and last working day of the month). When a payday falls on a weekend or holiday, paychecks will be distributed on the last working day prior to the weekend or holiday.

Leading Edge Agency

You are paid every other Friday for work completed through the previous Saturday. Our payroll and holiday schedules are distributed annually.

Author's Comments

You are legally required to post your payday schedule where it will be visible to all employees.

Work Schedules

Author's Comments

I encourage employers to be as flexible as possible with work schedules. However, you should have a policy stating that you reserve the right to request a change in work schedule to prevent your being held hostage by too many different scheduling needs.

If you are considering creating an alternate work schedule for full-time employees, such as four 10-hour days, you should closely follow wage and hour law requirements for establishing such a schedule.

Creative Agency

Creative Agency's offices are normally open to the public, volunteers and visitors Monday through Friday from 9 a.m. to 5 p.m. Although the majority of our staff members work those hours, some may work alternative schedules based on arrangements with their manager.

Nonexempt staff members should not start work before their scheduled start time or work beyond their accustomed ending time without the prior approval of their manager.

By the Book Agency

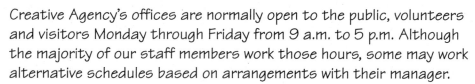

Employees of BBA are expected to work the number of hours agreed upon at the time of hire.

Although the regular workweek is from 9 a.m. to 5 p.m. Monday through Friday, other work arrangements may be made between the employee and his/her supervisor, subject to the demands and limitations of the job and department. Supervisors have final approval for flex-time requests, and retain the authority to require the employee to return to a regular schedule, should organizational need require it.

Leading Edge Agency

Work schedules at LEA are based on department/facility functions and individual job responsibilities. Work schedules may vary from department to department and employee to employee. All schedules are subject to change and require a manager's approval.

Full-time employees are expected to work an average of 40 hours per week.

FLEX-TIME

We recognize that we can accomplish our organizational goals and support employees' family and personal responsibilities by making it possible for you to work a schedule that does not conform to our regular hours of operation. We encourage you to use flex-time when it can accommodate both personal and agency needs. Flex-time requirements are as follows:

- Work must be suitable to flex-time scheduling

- The flex-time schedule will not inconvenience co-workers

- You have your manager's approval

Meal and Rest Periods

Creative Agency

All nonexempt staff members receive a paid ten-minute rest period for each four hours worked, or major fraction thereof. Full-time staff members should take one rest period in the first half of their day and one in the second half.

Nonexempt staff members who work five hours or more receive an unpaid lunch break of 30 minutes. Rest periods cannot be combined with the lunch break, but staff members may take up to a one-hour lunch break if desired. Staff members may not skip rest and meal breaks to shorten the workday.

By the Book Agency

(see policy outlined above)

Leading Edge Agency

We maintain an informal atmosphere and do not have a formal system for scheduling breaks during the workday. All employees are encouraged to pause during the workday to rest and give the eyes, hands, mouth and ears a break.

Nonexempt employees are required to take a paid 15-minute break during each four-hour block of work. Additionally, nonexempt employees must take a half-hour paid lunch break, and have the option of taking an additional unpaid half-hour.

We ask that all employees coordinate lunch and rest breaks with co-workers to ensure adequate coverage for all functions.

If you are nonexempt (entitled to overtime pay), you may not skip your breaks or meal period, nor can you combine breaks with lunch. It's the law!

Author's Comments

The law does not allow a nonexempt employee to combine paid breaks with a lunch hour or to skip breaks in order to leave earlier in the day. You are not required to pay nonexempt employees for lunch breaks, although some nonprofits choose to do so.

Nonexempt employees who are required to do any work (such as answering phones or remaining in the office) during their lunch break must be paid for this time.

Timekeeping Requirements

Creative Agency

All staff members must complete a time sheet for each pay period. Nonexempt staff members should record actual hours worked plus all use of paid time off. Exempt staff members need only track use of paid days off.

By the Book Agency

All employees submit time sheets for each pay period. Nonexempt employees record actual hours worked and leave taken, and exempt employees record leave taken. Any falsification of a time sheet will result in disciplinary action, up to and including discharge.

Leading Edge Agency

(see policies outlined above)

Overtime Pay

Creative Agency

Overtime is paid to nonexempt staff members according to federal and state law. Exempt staff members are not eligible for overtime pay. Overtime hours must be approved in advance by your manager.

Only hours actually worked are used to compute overtime earnings. Paid time off, such as holidays or vacation time, is not used to compute overtime.

By the Book Agency **BBA**

Nonexempt employees are paid at the rate of one and one-half times their regular rate of pay for hours worked in excess of 40 in a workweek.

Overtime is not at the employee's discretion; it requires advance supervisory approval. BBA does not provide compensatory time off as a substitute for overtime pay. Vacation, holiday and sick time do not constitute hours worked for the purposes of computing overtime.

Ordinarily, exempt employees are not compensated for working more than 40 hours in a week. In unusual circumstances, when an exempt employee is required to work a substantial number of extra hours, compensatory paid time off may be granted by the supervisor. Such time must be taken within 30 days of the extra time worked.

Leading Edge Agency

(see policies outlined above)

Author's Comments

The California legislature recently changed the state's overtime pay requirements. Effective January 1, 1998, California employers no longer pay overtime to nonexempt employees for hours worked in excess of eight in one day. Overtime pay is now required only for hours worked in excess of 40 in a workweek.

All California employers are required to post the Industrial Welfare Commission Orders governing wage and hour regulations.

Salary Advances

A salary advance can be given when a staff member is scheduled to take a vacation, up to the amount already accrued and scheduled for use during the vacation.

All Agencies

A salary advance can be given when a staff member is scheduled to take a vacation, up to the amount already accrued and scheduled for use during the vacation.

A salary advance for any other reason requires approval of the executive director and will be granted only in emergency situations. Any staff member receiving a salary advance (other than for vacation) must pay back the entire advance through payroll deductions within 30 days of receiving the advance.

Salary advances for any reason are limited to three per calendar year.

Wage Garnishments

All Agencies

From time to time we may be required to withhold monies from an employee's pay. If this agency receives a court-authorized garnishment or levy, the impacted staff member will be notified immediately.

Payroll Deductions

Creative Agency

Your payroll and earnings deductions are detailed with your check. Mandated and voluntary deductions usually include:

Mandated by federal and state law	Voluntary
federal income tax	health insurance
state income tax	Flexible Spending Account
Social Security tax/Medicare tax	savings
state disability insurance	repayment of salary advance
workers' compensation insurance	United Way contributions
garnishments/wage attachments	

Any questions about your paycheck should be directed to the director of finance.

By the Book Agency

(see policy outlined above)

Leading Edge Agency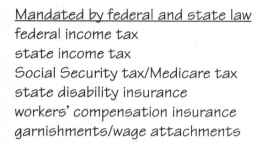

Attached to your paycheck is a pay stub showing the number of hours you worked during the pay period, the amount of your total earnings, specific contributions to benefit plans and the amounts of specific deductions as required by law or authorized by you. We suggest that you review your pay stub carefully each pay period and that you retain it for your records. If you have any questions about your deductions, please contact the payroll coordinator in our Finance Department.

Author's Comments

It is helpful to include this type of policy statement in your handbook because many employees are confused by the bite taken out of their paycheck by mandatory deductions. It's also a good idea to identify someone in your organization with whom employees can discuss their options for voluntary deductions and the impact of deductions on their paycheck.

Salary Philosophy

Author's Comments

It is beyond the scope of this handbook to cover salary administration policies and practices, but these are reviewed in depth in **The Management Center's** *Nonprofit Guide to Developing and Administering Sound Compensation Policies,* **which has been designed as a companion volume to this handbook.**

Creative Agency

At Creative Agency we strive for fairness and equity in all our policies and practices, including those that affect compensation. We offer a compensation package (your annual salary plus benefits) that reflects competitiveness in the marketplace and concern for our staff members' ability to balance their work and personal lives.

By the Book Agency

It is the policy of BBA to make every effort to compensate employees fairly and equitably, and to recognize the contributions made by existing employees as its highest priority in budgeting expenses.

The Board of Directors sets the salary of the executive director. All other salaries are set by the executive director, based on ranges approved by the board. Periodically, the executive director reviews salaries for all positions and utilizes information about compensation at other agencies to ensure that BBA remains competitive in its compensation practices.

Leading Edge Agency

It is important to us, as leaders in our community, that our compensation levels reflect the outstanding capabilities of our employees. The primary objective of our compensation program is to encourage and reinforce the attraction and retention of talented and dedicated employees.

Compensation ranges are reviewed annually and are designed to reflect competitiveness and equity based on internal and external factors. If you have questions or concerns about your salary level, you are encouraged to speak frankly with your manager or to meet with a member of our Human Resources staff.

Salary Reviews

Creative Agency

Staff members have the opportunity for a salary increase annually at the time of their anniversary of hire, or 12 months from their most recent salary review. Increases are not automatic, but are based on overall job performance and agency budget. Staff members who are on written warnings are not eligible for salary increases until their performance or other job-related issues are satisfactorily resolved.

By the Book Agency

(see policy outlined above)

Leading Edge Agency

All employees receive a compensation review as part of their annual performance evaluation process, which takes place at the end of the fiscal year. Employees must have been employed for at least six months to be eligible for an increase; increases given after more or less than 12 months of employment are prorated.

LEA grants salary increases on the basis of job performance, and increases are never guaranteed. Our pay-for-performance program is designed as an incentive, to reward outstanding job performance. We consider the following factors when determining a performance-based salary increase:

- Budget available for increases. Guidelines for salary increases are issued annually to reflect current budget capabilities

- Employee's overall job performance over the previous 12 months

- Performance of employee's entire department or work group in meeting annual objectives

- Employee's salary in relation to comparable salaries in like positions inside the organization

- Changes in the cost of living

In addition, you may receive a salary increase if you are promoted or given substantially new responsibilities, or if it is determined that your salary level is not equitable in comparison with that of others in like positions with similar levels of seniority.

Author's Comments

If yours is a larger organization, with opportunities for promotion and internal transfers, it is helpful to have a policy that stipulates how a promotional pay increase will affect an employee's annual salary review. If salary reviews are done on an anniversary-of-hire basis, then a mid-year promotion should change the salary review date.

AIDS and Other Life-Threatening Illnesses

Creative Agency

(not common practice)

By the Book Agency

(not common practice)

Author's Comments

A growing number of organizations have found it helpful to have a specific policy to address treatment of employees with HIV/AIDS and other life-threatening diseases. Creating such a policy is one good step toward eliminating bias and misconceptions about the abilities of individuals with life-threatening diseases to continue to be productive employees.

We believe that a

supportive and caring

work environment

is an important

factor in maintaining

quality of life

for an employee

with a life-threatening

illness.

Leading Edge Agency

At LEA we believe employees with life-threatening illnesses (including, but not limited to cancer, HIV/AIDS, heart disease and multiple sclerosis) should continue to work for as long as their condition allows them to do so in a safe and satisfactory manner.

We believe that a supportive and caring work environment is an important factor in maintaining quality of life for an employee with a life-threatening illness. We ask all our employees to be sensitive to the needs of colleagues facing such an illness. Managers should provide ill employees with referrals to available services and assist them with personal support appropriate to the work environment.

Upon request, LEA will provide reasonable accommodation to employees with a life-threatening illness to enable them to continue to work. Such accommodation might include flexible schedules to accommodate medical treatments and tasks that do not require physical exertion.

Through continuing education and communication we will attempt to create a supportive, open and informed work environment in which anyone with a life-threatening illness will feel free to come forward in the knowledge that s/he will be met with respect, understanding and care.

An employee with a life-threatening illness is under no obligation to disclose her/his condition to LEA. If an employee chooses to discuss a life-threatening illness, any such conversation will be considered strictly confidential and will not be disclosed to others without the employee's permission (except as required by law). Unauthorized disclosure of confidential information relating to health status will lead to disciplinary action, up to and including dismissal.

Employees with AIDS or HIV are entitled to the full range of medical insurance and disability benefits provided for employees with life-threatening illnesses.

Punctuality and Attendance

Creative Agency

We expect staff members to arrive at work on time and to work their full weekly schedule. If you need to be absent from work for any reason, you must call your supervisor before the start of your workday and, if possible, leave a message the night before.

By the Book Agency

BBA

Employees who are unable to report for work for any reason must notify their immediate supervisor within one hour of their regularly scheduled starting time.

In general, all employees are expected to be responsible and demonstrate respect for fellow employees by establishing a record of punctuality and regular attendance. These are factors considered in evaluating overall job performance.

Repetitive lateness and/or excessive absenteeism may result in disciplinary action up to and including termination.

Leading Edge Agency

(see policies outlined above)

Author's Comments

When crafting a policy about punctuality and attendance, it is important to be very specific about notification. Spell out exactly when an employee is expected to notify her/his supervisor of lateness or absence, so your agency can avoid a mad scramble for coverage.

Use of Facilities and Property

Creative Agency

Respect for and protection of staff members' personal property and CA's facilities and property is everyone's responsibility. If you find property missing or damaged, please notify our office manager immediately.

BBA

By the Book Agency

Employees are asked to treat agency property as they would their own. Specifically, employees are to keep their own work area and common areas clean and well-maintained, and limit their use of agency equipment to work-related purposes. Employees are required to receive supervisory approval before removing any agency property from the premises.

Occasionally, employees may need to enter agency premises after the offices are closed to retrieve personal items or to complete projects. Employees must provide their supervisor with advance notice if they intend to enter the premises after office hours.

Leading Edge Agency

(see policies outlined above)

> **Employees are to keep their own work area and common areas clean and well-maintained, and limit their use of agency equipment to work-related purposes.**

Guests and Visitors

Creative Agency
(not common practice)

By the Book Agency
(not common practice)

Leading Edge Agency

(LEA)

Please keep visits from friends and family to a minimum, in order to preserve an appropriate work environment. We provide a number of opportunities throughout the year for friends and family to visit our workplace, and visits are best made during those times.

We provide a number of opportunities throughout the year for friends and family to visit our workplace, and visits are best made during those times.

Keys and Security

Creative Agency
(not applicable: size)

By the Book Agency
(not applicable: size)

Leading Edge Agency

(LEA)

LEA strives to provide a secure work environment for our employees, volunteers, clients and visitors. We provide for the security of our buildings and facilities by maintaining alarms and outside security services. We ask that you comply with all security procedures established in your work area, and that you immediately report any breach of security to your manager.

We encourage employees to be prudent about bringing personal items to work. LEA is not responsible for losses resulting from theft of property while you are away from your work area.

Immediately report lost or stolen keys or other agency to your supervisor. Copying or giving keys, or lock combinations, to an unauthorized individual will be considered grounds for immediate dismissal.

Author's Comments

A security policy does not take the place of security measures and procedures. Depending on your organization's location and facilities, you may want to provide specific training on security procedures.

Personal Use of Phones

Author's Comments

It is inevitable that phones will be used for personal business to some extent. The most important aspect of a phone use policy is to require the use of personal calling cards for long distance calls.

Creative Agency

Although occasional personal phone calls are to be expected, please confine your use of the phones to agency business as much as possible. Should circumstances require that you place a long-distance call, we ask that you use a personal calling card or call collect.

By the Book Agency

(see policy outlined above)

Leading Edge Agency

The telephone is one of our most important service tools. Please be certain that your phone manner reflects care and courtesy toward our clients and the public. Except in cases of emergency, please keep personal phone calls brief and infrequent.

Personal Automobile Use

All Agencies

Employees who use their own automobiles for travel on authorized agency business will be reimbursed for mileage at the rate established by the IRS. Employees must have prior supervisory approval for the use of personal vehicles and must carry, at their own expense, the minimum insurance coverage for property damage and public liability.

Attire and Personal Hygiene

All Agencies

It is expected that employees will maintain a clean and neat appearance and will project a professional and businesslike image in dealing with other employees, clients, volunteers and the general public. This agency reserves the right to define appropriate standards of appearance for the workplace.

Expense Reimbursement

Creative Agency

Staff members are reimbursed for approved travel and entertainment expenses. Staff members are asked to complete a record of all expenses for which they seek reimbursement and to submit receipts along with the expense record for reimbursement. Reimbursement is made via check within two weeks of receipt of the reimbursement request.

By the Book Agency

BBA

Reasonable and customary personal expenses incurred in the performance of one's job will be reimbursed. Reimbursement requires prior authorization by the employee's immediate supervisor, approval of actual expenses and completion of a signed, itemized voucher.

Leading Edge Agency

(see policies outlined above)

Author's Comments

Requirements for dress and appearance vary greatly from one organization to another, based not only on the amount of contact your employees have with clients, supporters and the general public, but on the image of the organization as well. Generally, the more your employees interact with outsiders, the more you need a policy governing dress and cleanliness.

If you intend to restrict your employees' dress, or to prohibit certain types of attire or jewelry (for instance, nose rings, baseball caps or shorts), be certain that you have a bona fide job-based reason for doing so. Many people guard their independence fiercely these days, and are willing to take a stand for their right to look unique.

Confidentiality of Voice Mail and Electronic Mail

Author's Comments

More and more organizations are using voice mail and E-mail for interoffice communications. While you do not want your employees to feel that Big Brother is watching them, you do need to inform them of the instances in which it may be necessary to review computer records or messages they have sent. Encourage employees to use computers, E-mail and voice mail for work-related activities only.

Creative Agency

(see policies outlined below)

By the Book Agency

BBA

BBA employees use voice mail and electronic mail to communicate with others in the agency and to receive messages when they are unavailable. Employees should be aware that voice mail and electronic mail messages are not private and are subject to review by the agency in the case of an investigation of unlawful activity or violations of agency policy.

Time spent online on an agency-sponsored account should concern BBA business only. Excessive personal use of an online E-mail account may result in a request for reimbursement or cancellation of access to the account or to E-mail.

Leading Edge Agency

LEA recognizes that its employees have reasonable expectations of privacy with regard to the use of voice mail and E-mail, even when this use is restricted to LEA business and the information is stored in LEA computers.

LEA reserves the right to access and disclose the contents of employee voice mail and E-mail messages, but will only do so when it has a legitimate business need and the urgency of the need is sufficiently strong to offset the organization's commitment to employee privacy.

LEA does not and will not monitor voice mail and E-mail messages as a routine matter. LEA may inspect the contents of voice mail and E-mail messages or information stored on computers in the course of an investigation into improper or unlawful behavior or as necessary to locate substantive information that is not readily available by some other means. LEA may disclose a voice mail or E-mail message or information stored on computer to law enforcement officials if the organization has reason to believe that it may have been the victim of a crime or is legally obligated to do so.

Electronic "snooping" by any employee is a violation of LEA policy and grounds for disciplinary action up to and including dismissal. We do not take the inspection of voice mail, E-mail and computer records lightly, and any request for access to such information must be approved in advance by the executive director.

Employee Information

Creative Agency

(see policies outlined below)

By the Book Agency

BBA

It is important that personnel files contain up-to-date information regarding each employee. Employees should inform their supervisor immediately whenever there are changes in their personal data, such as address, telephone number, marital status, domestic partnership, number of dependents and person to notify in case of emergency.

Employees have the right to inspect their personnel file during regular office hours, given reasonable notice to the agency. An appointment to inspect the file may be made with the director of operations, who will accompany the employee while he/she inspects his/her file. Employees may obtain copies of any document in their personnel file to the extent required by law. Personnel records are the property of BBA and are not allowed to leave the office of the director of operations without authorization.

No reference information other than a verification of dates of employment, wage and title(s) will be given out to a third party without prior written authorization by the employee.

Leading Edge Agency

LEA

Your individual personnel file is kept in the Human Resources Department. If you want to review its contents you may make an appointment to do so at any time during normal operating hours. A member of the Human Resources staff must be present when you review your file, and files may not be removed from the Human Resources Department. You may, however, obtain copies of any document in your file.

Your personnel file is treated as confidential by LEA. The information it contains is available to you, your manager, the Human Resources staff, the executive director, and others as required by law or organizational necessity. Our policy with prospective employers is to verify an employee's position, dates of employment and salary only.

We will not, under any circumstances, give out your home phone number or address unless you specifically request that we do so, or we are required to do so by law.

Agency Confidentiality

Author's Comments

It's particularly important for social service organizations working directly with clients to establish a confidentiality policy.

If your organization works with sensitive or proprietary information on a regular basis, you may want to have employees sign a confidentiality agreement, in addition to having a confidentiality policy.

Creative Agency

Confidential information obtained during or through employment with Creative Agency may not be used by any staff member for the purpose of furthering current or future outside employment or activities, or for obtaining personal gain or profit.

At no time should a staff member disclose nonpublic or sensitive information to individuals other than on a need-to-know basis.

By the Book Agency

(see the policy outlined below)

Leading Edge Agency

All records, history and discussions about the people we serve must be considered private and kept in confidence. The very fact that an individual is served by LEA can only be disclosed under specified conditions, which are described below, for reasons relating to law enforcement and fulfillment of our mission.

Employees may not disclose any information about a person, including the fact that the person is or is not served by our organization, to anyone outside this organization unless authorized by the executive director or other authorized personnel. The principle of confidentiality must be maintained in all programs, departments, functions and activities.

Information about clients of LEA can only be disclosed under the following circumstances:

1. If a release-of-information form is explained to and completed by the person the information is about before it is released.

2. If records are inspected by an outside agency. The individuals who inspect records must be specifically authorized to do so by the executive director. The taking of notes and copying or removal of records are specifically prohibited in such cases.

3. The only other instance in which client information will be released to a person outside the agency is when we are required to do so by law.

Employees are specifically instructed not to release to state, federal or other agencies information about any individuals or their records that would enable any person served to be identified by name, address, Social Security number or other coding procedures, unless the employee is authorized to do so by the executive director. Failure to follow these client confidentiality procedures will be grounds for immediate dismissal.

All records, history

and discussions

about the people

we serve must

be considered

private and kept

in confidence.

Speaking to the Media

Creative Agency

(see policies outlined below)

By the Book Agency

BBA

BBA has designated the director of communications as the person responsible for speaking with the press and making written and oral statements for publication. Any request for information or interviews by the media should be referred to the director of communications or the executive director.

Leading Edge Agency

LEA

It is our goal to give the press a clear, consistent and up-to-date message about our organization and its programs and services. Since information about our activities changes often, it is easy to give the press information that is inaccurate or misleading.

Please refer all calls from newspapers, magazines or radio and television reporters to our vice president for public affairs or to the executive director.

> ## Author's Comments
>
> **A media relations policy is particularly useful in times of trouble – for instance, in the advent of budget cuts or changes in senior management It also helps to ensure that you are putting out a consistent message about your programs and services.**
>
> **Please refer all calls from newspapers, magazines or radio and television reporters to our vice president for public affairs or to the executive director.**

Internal Communication

Creative Agency

We use bulletin boards, mail boxes and office E-mail to communicate important information to staff members on a regular basis. Each of our staff members is responsible for reading posted or distributed information on a timely basis.

By the Book Agency

(see policy outlined above)

To encourage

understanding

and dialogue about

our organization

among all employees,

we provide a number

of formal vehicles

to facilitate

communication

throughout LEA.

Leading Edge Agency

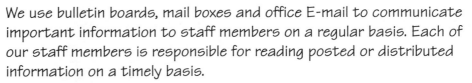

At LEA we believe that frequent, open communication of information about our operations, programs and activities is an essential ingredient in maintaining a productive working environment. To encourage understanding and dialogue about our organization among all employees, we provide a number of formal vehicles to facilitate communication throughout LEA.

We publish a **newsletter** once a month — employees who wish to contribute to the newsletter are encouraged to contact the Human Resources Department. Our Human Resources Department also publishes a weekly **E-mail** update, highlighting current activities and events. We maintain **bulletin boards** throughout our facilities for posting memos, job openings and information about your rights as an employee. Lastly, we hold quarterly **all-staff meetings** to provide an opportunity for all employees to hear directly from members of our senior management team about our progress toward annual goals.

LEA reserves the right to determine what may be posted on bulletin boards and to remove notices that are outdated or inappropriate for our work environment.

We expect you to read published and posted information and to attend meetings in order to keep informed about our activities and the opportunities that are available to you.

Solicitations

Creative Agency

No soliciting is allowed on agency premises. This includes requests for contributions to charitable organizations, as well as business advertising and the sale of goods (Girl Scout cookies, Tupperware, etc.).

By the Book Agency

BBA

Solicitations and distributions are not permitted, except for annual charitable campaigns (such as United Way) that are formally approved by the Board of Directors. Examples of activities that are not permitted include:

- Solicitation by an employee during his or her work time

- Solicitation by an employee not on work time of another employee who is on work time

- Any solicitation or distribution by nonemployees

- Distribution of advertising materials or literature of any kind in work areas

For the purposes of this policy, the following definitions apply:

- Solicitation includes, but is not limited to, any request for signatures, contributions, support of political activities, merchandise purchases and organizing activities

- Distribution includes, but is not limited to, passing out of literature, pamphlets, leaflets or notices of any kind

- Work time means all hours an employee is or should be working other than lunch or break time

- Work areas are any area where BBA work is regularly performed

Leading Edge Agency

LEA

We do not permit solicitation, money collection or the sale of merchandise by one employee to another while either employee is on work time. By "work time" we mean all time on our premises, in travel to or from one of our facilities or on agency business, other than meal periods and break times.

We likewise prohibit the distribution of literature, and the circulation of petitions or advertisements at any time. Finally, soliciting or distributing any literature by a nonemployee is prohibited on all LEA property.

Harassment

Author's Comments

Due to a U.S. Supreme Court ruling in November 1993, employers are now responsible for ensuring that the workplace is free of factors that can create a "hostile working environment," in which a reasonable person would find it difficult to do her or his work. Do not allow sexual joking, innuendoes or sexually offensive comments or visual materials in your offices or work facilities.

It is important to state that all complaints will be promptly investigated and that no retaliation will be taken against any employee who files a complaint in good faith.

It is not enough to simply have a policy against harassment – you should also provide some sort of consistent education or training for all your employees about what constitutes harassment and how to prevent it in your workplace.

Creative Agency

It is illegal to harass others on the basis of their sex, sexual orientation, age, race, color, national origin, religion, marital or veteran status, citizenship, disability or other personal characteristics. Harassment includes making derogatory remarks about such characteristics, making jokes about ethnic or other groups and other verbal, physical and visual behavior.

Sexual harassment is also prohibited. Propositions, repeated requests for dates, dirty jokes, sexually provocative pictures or cartoons and other verbal, physical and visual harassment of a sexual nature are prohibited. The harassment of any staff member will lead to immediate disciplinary action up to and including termination.

Any staff member who feels harassed has the right to file a charge with the Equal Employment Opportunity Commission, and with a state agency. Before doing so, we ask that you first speak with your manager. If your manager is not appropriate, then speak with our executive director or a member of the board's Personnel Committee, so that appropriate internal action may be taken. It is the responsibility of all managers to listen to such complaints and to refer them to the appropriate authority. We will not retaliate against any staff member who makes a claim of harassment.

By the Book Agency

BBA

It is the policy of the agency that there shall be no harassment of any employee by fellow employees or by any supervisor on account of an employee's sex, race, national origin, religion, physical handicap or sexual preference (or on account of any other protected status).

The agency does not condone and will not permit such harassment of any employee and, in particular, will not tolerate the making of unwelcome sexual advances to any employee, unwelcome physical, verbal or visual behavior that is sexual in nature or the making of remarks or jokes known to be offensive to any employee because of his/her sex, age, race, national origin, religion, physical handicap or sexual preference. If an employee believes he/she has been treated in violation of this policy, he/she should immediately report the matter to the chair of the Personnel Committee. The Personnel Committee will seek to promptly investigate all complaints or violations of this policy in as discreet a manner as possible.

Leading Edge Agency

(see policies outlined above)

Workplace Conduct

Creative Agency

We have developed certain guidelines to reflect what we believe are good business practices. We strive to develop and maintain a pleasant, efficient and fair work environment that fosters cooperation and understanding.

All staff members are expected to be:

- On time and ready for work at the beginning of their workday
- Careful and conscientious in the performance of their work
- Respectful and considerate of others
- Courteous and helpful, both when dealing with other staff members and with volunteers, supporters and the general public

By the Book Agency

BBA

Every organization has certain guidelines, which are developed to reflect sound operational practices. BBA requires discipline, cooperation, efficiency and productivity of its employees. BBA has standards of behavior with which all employees are required to comply. Failure to comply with these standards will result in disciplinary action, up to and including termination. Examples of conduct that may require disciplinary action include, but are not limited to:

- Substandard job performance
- Failure to carry out job responsibilities
- Being absent from work without prior notification to supervisor
- Safety violation(s)
- Excessive tardiness or absenteeism
- Unauthorized overtime
- Rudeness or discourtesy toward a fellow employee, supervisor, volunteer, supporter or member of the general public

Leading Edge Agency

(LEA)

All employees at LEA share responsibility for observing certain standards of conduct. These standards emphasize personal and professional integrity in all activities. Generally, treating others with the respect and consideration with which you expect to be treated and maintaining open, ongoing communication with your manager and co-workers will create a basis for a successful work experience.

It is the obligation and responsibility of each employee at LEA to work on resolving problems and conflicts by focusing on solutions and keeping issues work-related (as opposed to personal), and by communicating directly with the person or persons with whom you have a conflict. In most cases, discussing a situation will clear it up.

Author's Comments

The primary purpose of any employee handbook is to establish clear expectations: both of what you expect from an employee, and of what an employee can expect from your organization as a place of employment. A Workplace Conduct section is the place where you can put across your basic expectations of professional behavior and the ways in which your organization will deal with performance and conduct problems. Take advantage of this opportunity to clearly articulate your standards and your organization's disciplinary philosophy. (See page 106 for further employee expectations.)

Open-Door Policy

Author's Comments

Most organizations operate with an informal open-door policy, meaning that employees are encouraged to speak frankly to their supervisor or other appropriate members of management about job-related concerns.

Creative Agency

All staff members are encouraged to provide input and suggestions concerning the overall operations and programs of Creative Agency, following appropriate communication channels. Staff members should initially bring their comments to their own manager. When that may be inappropriate, staff members may speak directly with the executive director.

We operate in an open-door manner. All input from staff will be considered and can be presented without fear of personal recrimination.

By the Book Agency

BBA

BBA has an open-door policy that encourages employee participation in decisions that will affect them and their daily professional responsibilities. This policy also encourages employees who have job-related problems or complaints to talk them over with their supervisor or a manager at any level of management who they feel can help them. BBA believes that employee concerns are best addressed through informal and open communication.

BBA will attempt to keep all such expressions of concern, their investigation and the terms of their resolution confidential. However, in the course of investigating and resolving concerns, some dissemination of information to others may be appropriate.

No employee will be disciplined or otherwise penalized for raising a concern in good faith.

BBA has an open-door policy that encourages employee participation in decisions that will affect them and their daily professional responsibilities.

Leading Edge Agency

(see policies outlined above)

Disciplinary Procedures

Creative Agency

DISCIPLINARY ACTION

The primary objective of any disciplinary action is to improve job performance. Actions by a staff member that are inappropriate for the work environment, are a hindrance to effective job performance or violate agency policy constitute improper conduct and may be cause for disciplinary action.

Creative Agency maintains a progressive and participatory disciplinary system, which may include all or some of the following steps:

1. Documented oral warning
2. Written warning
3. Final written warning
4. Suspension
5. Dismissal

Based on circumstances, a manager may choose to enter into disciplinary action at any step in the process, including immediate dismissal. All disciplinary action beyond oral warning requires the approval of the executive director.

Author's Comments

Regardless of the specifics of your organization's approach to discipline, you should have a disciplinary process that is generally progressive in nature. Just as important, you should state that some problems will result in immediate termination, and that it is at management's discretion to decide what step in a disciplinary process is most appropriate.

Disciplinary Procedures, continued

Discipline may be required for substandard job performance, safety violations, absenteeism or inability to work as part of a team.

By the Book Agency

BBA

CORRECTIVE ACTION

The corrective action process is designed to protect the safety and promote the fair treatment of all employees. Discipline may be required for substandard job performance, safety violations, absenteeism or inability to work as part of a team. BBA supervisors are responsible for identifying problems and assisting in their resolution. Any discipline involving suspension or discharge must be reviewed and approved by the executive director.

There are three levels of corrective action, any one of which may be entered into, depending upon the circumstances and severity of the problem:

1. **Employee Counseling or Verbal Warning**

   Employee is counseled by the supervisor following a minor offense in an effort to eliminate possible misunderstandings and to identify what constitutes good performance. The supervisor will help the employee to develop a solution and to improve performance to the appropriate level. Verbal warnings are documented by the supervisor and signed by the employee.

2. **Written Warning**

   Employee meets with supervisor and is presented with a written notice of corrective action. A written warning is designed to make sure that the employee is fully aware of the misconduct or performance problem, including the degree of seriousness and the consequences if the problem is not corrected. The supervisor and employee set a time frame during which improvement must be made and maintained, and a check-in process is determined. Employees on written warning are not eligible for promotions, transfers or pay increases unless specifically approved by the executive director.

3. **Discharge**

   In cases of serious misconduct, immediate rather than progressive corrective action may be taken. Termination can result from a single serious offense, or it can be the final step in a process to correct a series of minor offenses of the same nature. It can also occur as the result of ongoing conduct that is inconsistent with BBA policy.

   An employee may be suspended with pay pending an investigation of a charge of serious misconduct.

Disciplinary Procedures, continued

Leading Edge Agency

PERFORMANCE IMPROVEMENT

Occasionally, it becomes necessary for you and your manager to formally address a problem by identifying unacceptable behavior and establishing a clear plan for correcting it. This usually occurs after informal attempts to resolve the situation have failed.

This process is called performance improvement. It is a progressive process extending from a formal performance counseling session with your manager, through a written Performance Improvement Plan, to termination of employment. This process is designed to facilitate clear, precise and timely communication about problems and the development of solutions.

Employees who are in the performance improvement process are not eligible for raises, promotions or transfers until the process has been satisfactorily completed. While performance improvement is usually a progressive process, managers may choose to move to any step in the process, including immediate termination of employment, based on the severity of the problem or misconduct and the circumstances.

Some examples of conduct that may require beginning the formal performance improvement process are:

- Substandard job performance

- Failure to carry out job responsibilities

- Inability to work effectively with others

- Excessive absenteeism or tardiness

- Unauthorized overtime

Managers are required to enlist the support of the Human Resources Department when entering into the performance improvement process. Termination of employment requires the review and approval of the executive director.

Performance improvement... is a process designed to facilitate clear, precise and timely communication about problems and the development of solutions.

Complaint Procedures

Creative Agency

EMPLOYEE APPEAL PROCESS

As a matter of general policy, managers at all levels will provide an open door for discussion and a receptive ear, and will review all staff member suggestions or complaints concerning our work practices and procedures.

If a staff member wishes to make a formal complaint, it should be done within a reasonable time after the incident or issue has occurred. We consider an open discussion between employee and manager as the first step of the complaint procedure. The manager must respond to the complaint in a timely manner. If the complaint is not resolved by the manager within a reasonable time frame, or if the staff member disagrees with the manager's solution, the staff member may appeal directly to the executive director.

At this point the complaint must be written down, with the nature of the grievance clearly outlined. The executive director will investigate the complaint and notify the staff member, in writing, of her/his decision within a reasonable amount of time.

As a last resort, a staff member may take her/his complaint to the Personnel Committee of the Board of Directors. The Personnel Committee's decision constitutes the agency's final word on the matter.

By the Book Agency

GRIEVANCE PROCEDURE

Any employee who has a complaint concerning a BBA policy or its application has the right to file a grievance according to procedures outlined in this policy. No employee will be discriminated against, harassed or intimidated, or suffer any reprisal as a result of filing a grievance or participating in the investigation of a grievance. If an employee feels that he or she is being subjected to any reprisal, that employee has the right to appeal directly to the executive director.

Employees should attempt to resolve the problem informally with their supervisor as soon as possible. If a solution cannot be reached, the employee may present a formal grievance, in writing, to the executive director.

All complaints will be handled in a timely manner. BBA's goal is to resolve a complaint within 20 working days from the time of its initiation. If an extension or reduction of the time limit becomes necessary, all parties involved will be notified. Employees may not file grievance procedures challenging the substance of a performance evaluation.

Complaint Procedures, continued

Leading Edge Agency

(LEA)

INTERNAL COMPLAINT REVIEW

The purpose of the internal complaint review is to provide all employees of LEA with the opportunity to seek internal resolution of their work-related complaints. This policy supplements the open-door policy set forth in this handbook, which states our philosophy that all employees have free access to their immediate supervisors or to other supervisors of their choice to informally express their work-related concerns.

We will attempt to treat all internal complaints and their investigation as confidential, recognizing, however, that in the course of investigating and resolving internal complaints some dissemination of information to others may be appropriate.

PROCEDURE

Written complaints should be directed to the executive director as soon as possible after the date of the event(s) that gave rise to the work-related concern, but no later than ten days following such event(s).

The executive director (or her/his designee) will set up a meeting to discuss the complaint within a reasonable time following the receipt of the written complaint. As necessary, the executive director (or her/his designee) will also meet with others who are named in the complaint or who may have knowledge of the facts set forth in the complaint.

Within ten working days of the meeting(s) described above, the executive director will provide the employee with a written response to her/his complaint. (This time frame may be changed according to circumstances.) If the complaint is resolved to the employee's satisfaction, the terms of the resolution will be recorded and signed by the employee and the executive director.

APPEAL

If the complaint is related to the termination of an employee, and if the employee is not satisfied with the decision of the executive director, the employee may take the matter to arbitration, but only if the employee agrees in writing that the arbitration decision will be final and may not be relitigated in court. If the employee agrees to arbitration as the final solution, LEA will pay the arbitrator's fee. Arbitrators will be selected in accordance with the rules of the American Arbitration Association. Inclusion of this arbitration provision is not intended to alter the at-will status of anyone's employment.

NONRETALIATION

No employee who has filed a complaint in good faith will be unlawfully disciplined or otherwise retaliated against, even if LEA does not agree with the complaint.

> This policy supplements the open-door policy set forth in this handbook, which states our philosophy that all employees have free access to their immediate supervisors or to other supervisors of their choice to informally express their work-related concerns.

Conflict of Interest

Author's Comments

A conflict of interest policy is an effective preventive measure. Often employees don't fully comprehend what does and does not constitute a conflict of interest unless you spell it out for them.

A conflict of interest is a situation in which an employee's private interest or outside economic interest interferes with the employee's duties and responsibilities at BBA or with BBA's general activities.

Creative Agency

We are proud of our reputation for conducting our activities with fairness and integrity. We require all our staff members to uphold this reputation in every work-related activity. If you are ever in doubt about whether an activity meets our high ethical standards or compromises our reputation, please discuss your concerns with your manager or our executive director.

By the Book Agency

It is important that employees avoid conflicts of interest to maintain high standards of conduct. A conflict of interest is a situation in which an employee's private interest or outside economic interest interferes with the employee's duties and responsibilities at BBA or with BBA's general activities.

Employees must advise the executive director of any outside employment (on either a salary or a fee basis). Any employee needing advice about a potential conflict of interest should consult with the director of operations or the executive director. If an employee's outside activity is determined to constitute a conflict of interest, and the activity continues beyond a reasonable amount of time, disciplinary action will result, up to and including termination of employment.

Leading Edge Agency

We expect all our employees to use good judgment, to adhere to high ethical standards and to avoid situations that create an actual or potential conflict of interest between the employee's interests and the interests of LEA. If you are unsure as to whether a certain transaction, activity or relationship, including outside employment, constitutes a conflict of interest, you should discuss it with our director of human resources or the director of operations. Any exceptions to this guideline must be approved in writing by our executive director.

We intend that this conflict of interest policy be interpreted fairly, so that we do not create harsh results when a conflict unavoidably arises. If an employee violates this policy through no fault of her or his own, or unintentionally, s/he will be given a reasonable amount of time (as determined by the executive director) to comply with our policy.

Nevertheless, you should know that failure to adhere to these guidelines, including failure to disclose any conflicts or to seek an exception, may result in discipline, up to and including termination of employment.

Fraternization

Creative Agency
(not applicable: size)

By the Book Agency
(not applicable: size)

Leading Edge Agency

LEA strictly prohibits employees from fraternizing with any of the people served by our programs. We also prohibit the transferring of money or goods between employees and persons currently or formerly served.

If evidence of nonprofessional, nonwork-related interaction between an employee and any person(s) served by LEA is found, we will conduct a thorough investigation to determine if there has been a violation of our fraternization policy. If a policy violation is proven, the employee will be dismissed, and a report will be filed with the appropriate authorities if vulnerable adults are involved.

Employees are further required to exercise good judgment in establishing nonprofessional, nonwork-related relationships with persons formerly served by our programs. In general, we discourage such relationships at any time. If you have a concern about a potential personal relationship with a former client, please discuss it in confidence with our director of human resources.

Author's Comments

Fraternization policies are a necessity for those organizations providing direct service to individuals in the community. Some nonprofit social service organizations hire and train individuals they formerly served, in which case a fraternization policy becomes even more essential. Make sure your employees understand that inappropriate relationships can undermine your programs or create the appearance of favoritism, and then make sure they know you will strictly enforce your fraternization policy.

Fees and Honoraria

Creative Agency

When staff members consult, lecture, counsel or advise outside individuals or organizations on behalf of CA, all fees, donations or cash honoraria must be paid to CA.

By the Book Agency

BBA

All requests for presentations relating to BBA are to be routed to the executive director, who will determine the appropriate person to represent the agency at the event. Any fee or honorarium provided is to be made payable to BBA.

Leading Edge Agency

(see policies outlined above)

> **All requests for presentations relating to BBA are to be routed to the executive director, who will determine the appropriate person to represent the agency at the event.**

Relations with Suppliers

Creative Agency

(see policies outlined below)

By the Book Agency

BBA

From time to time, employees may be offered gifts, entertainment or other favors from a supplier, contractor or organization with which BBA has business dealings. Beyond nominal gifts and common courtesies, no item of value can be accepted by an employee of BBA.

Furthermore, all employees should understand that entering into a personal relationship with a subordinate employee or with an employee of a supplier, contractor or other organization having financial dealings with BBA creates a possible conflict of interest that requires full disclosure to BBA.

Leading Edge Agency

(LEA)

While LEA encourages you to have friendly relations with suppliers and contractors, you must always base your business decisions solely on our organization's needs and the quality of the product or service supplied.

Generally, you should not accept gifts, favors, entertainment, free services or discounts on personal purchases or any other special considerations for yourself or your family. Gifts received from suppliers during the holidays should be shared with our entire staff.

All your dealings should be conducted in an open, honest, professional and completely ethical manner. If you have any questions about what may be perceived as ethical or unethical, please talk with your manager.

Author's Comments

Depending upon the frequency with which your organization does business with outside vendors and contractors, you may choose to include this policy or feel it isn't needed. I believe that setting clear limits on gifts from suppliers prevents problems from developing over time. Without reading such a policy, some employees may not even consider the possibility that they appear to be engaging in favoritism or inappropriate supplier relations.

At-Will Status

Creative Agency

We hope to retain good employees. However, employment at Creative Agency is for no specified time, regardless of length of service. Just as you are free to leave at any time, for any reason, we reserve the same right to end our employment relationship with you at any time, with or without notice, for any reason not prohibited by law.

No policy contained in this handbook should be interpreted as in any way changing your at-will status.

By the Book Agency

Employment with By the Book Agency is not for any specified period and can be terminated by either the employee or By the Book Agency at any time with or without any particular reason or advance notice. Nothing contained in these policies is intended to, or should be construed to, alter the at-will relationship between BBA and its employees. Although other terms and conditions and benefits of employment with BBA may change from time to time, the at-will relationship of employment is one aspect that cannot be changed except by an agreement in writing with the Board of Directors, signed by the chair of the board on behalf of the entire board.

Leading Edge Agency

At LEA we are committed to the philosophy that employment relationships are both personal and voluntary. By this we mean that, although we hope for mutually beneficial working relationships with our employees, we recognize that changing circumstances make it impossible to guarantee employment. Your employment with LEA has no specified duration, and either you or LEA may end the employment relationship whenever either of us believes it is best to do so, without consideration of cause or notice.

While we maintain and revise written and other personnel policies in order to adapt to changing organizational needs, our policy of voluntary employment relationships is not affected by any personnel policies or programs as may be in effect from time to time. The voluntary nature of our employment relationship may not be changed except by a separate written agreement specifically entered into for such purpose and signed by our board president.

Voluntary Termination of Employment

Author's Comments

Although employees are free to leave their jobs with no notice, it is effective to spell out your request that they give two weeks' notice. I also recommend that you spell out a job abandonment policy, so as to avoid misunderstandings if an employee disappears and then reappears expecting to continue working.

Creative Agency

Any staff member may voluntarily resign her/his position at any time and for any reason. We will also consider that you have resigned if you:

- Fail to return from an approved leave of absence on the specified return date
- Fail to report to work without notice for three consecutive days

All staff members are asked to give a minimum of two weeks' written notice of resignation. If a staff member is required to leave our employ before the duration of her/his notice (if, for example, a replacement is hired) the staff member will be paid for the two-week notice period.

Staff members are required to turn over all keys and other agency property to the office manager before leaving on their last day of work.

By the Book Agency

(see policy outlined above)

Leading Edge Agency

If you decide to resign from your job at LEA, we ask that you give a minimum of two weeks' notice. Please submit a letter of resignation to your manager.

You are considered to have resigned if you do not return from a leave of absence, turn down a comparable position offered upon return from a leave of absence or have an unexcused and/or unreported absence of two consecutive days.

Before leaving on your last day of work, you must return all agency property, including keys, credit cards, computer equipment and any other agency property or documents issued to you during the course of your employment.

Author's Comments

By listing numerous examples of unacceptable behavior that can be grounds for dismissal, you are providing clear guidelines for standards of behavior. Employees need to understand, in no uncertain terms, those actions and behaviors that will not be tolerated in your workplace.

Involuntary Termination

All Agencies

This agency reserves the right to terminate any employee at any time, with or without cause or notice. Generally, when an employee is believed, in the opinion of his/her supervisor, to have a job performance problem or to be engaging in behavior that is unacceptable or counterproductive, the employee will be given an opportunity to improve his/her performance or behavior to an acceptable level by means of a formal disciplinary action process. However, the following list, while not complete, gives examples of behavior that can result in immediate termination of employment:

- Breaching confidentiality

- Violating the drug- and alcohol-free workplace policy

- Theft — including, but not limited to, the removal of agency property or the property of another employee from agency premises without prior authorization

- Walking off the job without supervisory approval

- Working for another employer while on a leave of absence without the prior consent of this agency

- Fighting, roughhousing, abusive language or conduct that is hostile or disrespectful toward a co-worker, supervisor, board member, volunteer, or any person(s) associated with or served by this agency

- Disregarding established safety procedures; knowingly creating an unsafe work situation for self or co-worker

- Falsifying or altering records or time sheets

- Refusing to perform a work-related duty when directly instructed to do so by a supervisor or member of management

- Possessing weapons or firearms on this agency's property

- Unauthorized use or dissemination of proprietary information

- Violating this agency's equal opportunity or harassment policies

- Unauthorized use of agency property, including vehicles

All involuntary terminations require review by the executive director.

Job Elimination/Layoffs

Creative Agency

From time to time, we may need to lay off an employee as a result of reorganization, job elimination, funding changes or lack of work. Should such a termination be necessary, all affected staff members will be given as much advance notice as is possible and practical.

If you lose your job due to a layoff or reorganization, you will receive all accrued, unused vacation pay, plus one week of severance pay for each year of employment up to a maximum of eight weeks' pay. You also will be eligible for continuation of your benefits coverage, based on the specifics of COBRA. (See health insurance continuation policies in the Benefits section for more information.)

By the Book Agency   **BBA**

If it becomes necessary to reduce or change the composition of BBA's workforce, the executive director, in consultation with the Personnel Committee of the Board of Directors, will decide which jobs will be eliminated.

Regular full- and part-time employees who have worked at least one calendar year and whose positions are eliminated by a workforce reduction may receive a severance allowance. Generally, severance pay is equal to one week of pay for every full year of employment, to a maximum of 12 weeks' pay. BBA's exact severance policy will be set by the executive director, with approval of the board, at the time of a workforce reduction.

Author's Comments

Given the financial challenges of running a nonprofit, it is wise to include a layoff policy in your handbook. The larger and more structured your organization is, the more detailed and specific your policy should be. In general, employees are most concerned with notice, the decision-making process and severance pay policies.

Job Elimination/Layoffs, continued

Leading Edge Agency

Given the realities of the nonprofit sector, cutbacks or job reductions may be unavoidable due to changes in programs, funding changes or forces beyond our control. LEA will strive to minimize the negative impact on current employees if a reduction in the workforce becomes necessary.

In the case where a program may have to be reduced in size or eliminated entirely, LEA will reduce staff progressively, using the following steps:

1. Voluntary reductions in staff size. This includes employees who take early retirement, a leave of absence or a reduction in hours.

2. Attrition.

3. Possible elimination of part-time positions before full-time positions.

4. Transfer of employees to other vacant positions within our operations, provided the employee meets the minimum qualifications of the position.

5. When determining which regular employees are laid off, our executive director may implement a seniority system giving consideration to factors such as, but not limited to, the following:
   - Performance evaluations
   - Length of service
   - Job specialty, responsibilities and special skills
   - Supervisory input

All affected employees will receive notice of a layoff in writing from the executive director at least 30 days prior to the layoff date. Employees who receive shorter notice will receive pay in lieu of notice for the difference between receipt of actual notice and 30 days.

Laid off employees will be paid for any accrued, unused vacation time. Employees will also receive one week of severance pay for every full year of service. Laid off employees currently enrolled in LEA's health insurance program will be offered the opportunity to continue the same coverage for up to 18 months by paying the cost of the monthly premium.

Exit Interviews

Creative Agency
(not common practice)

By the Book Agency
(not common practice)

Leading Edge Agency

A member of our Human Resources staff meets with all regular employees on or before their last day of work. This exit interview is meant to provide employees with the opportunity to reflect on their experience at LEA and to offer comments, advice or suggestions pertaining to our work policies and practices.

Information shared during an exit interview will be treated as confidential and acted upon in an appropriate and timely manner.

Author's Comments

Exit interviews are an invaluable source of information about what is working and what needs improvement in your workplace. Employees are more likely to be candid when they are leaving (voluntarily) and you can encourage candor by ensuring that their comments will be kept confidential.

This exit interview is meant to provide employees with the opportunity to reflect on their experience at LEA and to offer comments, advice or suggestions pertaining to our work policies and practices.

Employee Acknowledgment

No policy in this

handbook should

be interpreted as

in any way changing,

altering or nullifying

our policy of

voluntary, at-will

employment.

All Agencies

Please read the following information and return this acknowledgment form to your direct supervisor for inclusion in your personnel file.

This handbook is provided to you for information and immediate reference. Because we are a dynamic and changing organization, policies included in this handbook are subject to unilateral change, revision, deletion or addition by this organization from time to time with or without prior notice.

No policy in this handbook should be interpreted as in any way changing, altering or nullifying our policy of voluntary, at-will employment. Your employment with this organization has no specified duration, and either you or the organization may terminate the employment relationship whenever either of us believes it is desirable to do so, without consideration of cause or notice. The at-will nature of our relationship may not be changed except by a separate written agreement specifically entered into for such purpose and signed by the board chair.

This is to acknowledge that I have received and read my copy of the handbook, am familiar with and understand its contents and agree to comply with its terms during my employment.

(Please print)

Name: _____

Date: _____

Title: _____

Signature: _____

About The Management Center

The Management Center is a leading resource for nonprofit management support in Northern California. Since 1977, we've been helping good causes manage better. Our mission is to help nonprofit organizations achieve their full potential; through effective consulting, training and information resources, we assist nonprofit leaders in strengthening their organizations and enhancing their community service. Our various activities include:

- Board and Organizational Development

- Human Resources Management

- Programs for Nonprofit Leaders

- Recognizing and Promoting Excellence

For more information, please don't hesitate to contact us at:

The Management Center
870 Market St., Suite 800
San Francisco, CA 94102
voice (415) 362-9735
fax (415) 362-4603
tmc@tmcenter.org
www.tmcenter.org

About the Author

Leyna Bernstein is a values-driven consultant and trainer with expertise in organizational development and human resources management. She has more than a decade of experience creating and implementing personnel policies for socially responsible companies combined with several years' experience in the nonprofit sector as a consultant, board member and volunteer.

She established the human resources function at The Nature Company and was part of the senior management team that grew the company from a local business to a national retail chain. At The Gap, Inc., Ms. Bernstein was responsible for managing employee relations for 750 people at the corporate headquarters. Her most recent corporate position was as vice president of Human Resources and Administration at Smith & Hawken, a company widely recognized as a leader in the socially responsible business movement.

Through her consulting firm, Bernstein-Albano Associates, Ms. Bernstein has provided consulting and training services to Bay Area nonprofits and locally owned businesses since 1993.

Through her work as a consultant with The Management Center, Ms. Bernstein has provided human resources expertise to dozens of Northern California nonprofits, both large and small. Ms. Bernstein serves as vice president of the Board of The Women's Philharmonic, and also serves on the board of the San Francisco Jewish Film Festival, where she chairs the Personnel Committee. In 1997, Ms. Bernstein and her husband, Peter Barnes, founded Mesa Refuge, a nonprofit writers' retreat in Point Reyes Station, California.

Reader Response Form

Author's Comments

We'd like to receive your comments about *Best Practices*. Your feedback will be incorporated into future editions. Please fill out the form at left (make a photocopy first) and fax it to us at (415) 362-4603 or mail it to: The Management Center, 870 Market St., Suite 800, San Francisco, CA 94102-2903.

1. Do you represent a nonprofit agency? ❑ yes ❑ no

2. How many staff members does your organization have? _____

3. What is your annual budget? _____

4. In general, which agency track did you choose to follow?
   ❑ Creative   ❑ By the Book   ❑ Leading Edge

5. Did you use *Best Practices* to:
   ❑ Write a new personnel handbook?
   ❑ Revise an existing personnel handbook?
   ❑ As a general human resources tool?
   ❑ Other _____

6. How successfully did the author fulfill your needs? Any suggestions for improvements?

   _____

   _____

7. Is the content of the book accurate? Complete? _____

   _____

8. Is the book well organized? Clear? Easy to follow? Effective? _____

   _____

9. Is the book written in a clear, readable style? _____

10. What other books on the topic have you read? How does this book differ? How is it better? Worse? _____

11. Overall book review (please circle one)   (low) 1   2   3   4   5 (high)

12. Additional comments: _____

Human Resources Assistance

From recruitment and hiring to evaluation and compensation, The Management Center is Northern California's foremost provider of human resources assistance to nonprofits. In addition to publishing this handbook, our services include:

HR Consulting Services

We've been helping good causes manage better since 1977 through professional consulting services. Our team of experienced consultants is available to help you with:
- Customization of *Best Practices*
- Team Building
- Performance management systems
- Compensation studies
- Board strategic planning
- Mediation
- Leadership management training

Opportunity NOCs

Launched in 1986, this weekly publication of nonprofit organization classifieds (NOCs) is Northern California's most comprehensive source of diverse employment opportunities in the fields of health, education, social services, the environment and the arts. We have regional affiliates with publications in Atlanta, Boston, Dallas, Los Angeles and Philadelphia, plus a new National Opportunity NOCs Web site at www.opportunitynocs.org.

TempExecs

Created by The Management Center, TempExecs offers an interim management service to place seasoned professionals with nonprofit organizations.

Executive Search Services

This program assists nonprofit organizations in conducting management searches. In addition to direct efforts, the program also utilizes consultants from the private business sector for executive searches.

Wage & Benefit Survey

The only survey of its kind in Northern California, the Wage & Benefit Survey is a comprehensive report of current salaries and benefits paid to nonprofit personnel. Published by The Management Center since 1979, the Survey is an essential tool for determining nonprofit compensation levels.

Compensation Guide

A companion to our annual *Wage & Benefit Survey*, this book, written by Fred Kohler, provides direction on how to use the Survey, how to implement fair compensation systems and how to administer and maintain these systems. *(available fall '98)*

HR SkillBuilders

These popular workshops help participants develop performance management, hiring and recruiting skills.

The Assessment Tool

One of our highlighted on-line Web services is The Assessment Tool. This interactive questionnaire allows nonprofits to evaluate their organization's managerial performance in eight areas. Stop by our Web site at www.tmcenter.org to test drive a module for free!

For More Information:

The Management Center
870 Market St., Suite 800
San Francisco, CA 94102
voice (415) 362-9735
fax (415) 362-4603
www.tmcenter.org
tmc@tmcenter.org

Best Practices: The Electronic Version

Copyright

Disclaimer

Neither the print nor electronic edition of *Best Practices: The Model Employee Handbook for California Nonprofits* is intended to be a substitute for experienced legal advice. Although we have attempted to cover most major issues regarding recent employment and labor law, it is not all-inclusive. The information provided herein is general in nature and the materials provided are exemplars only. This publication is not a do-it-yourself guide. The Management Center, Jossey-Bass and its associates do not guarantee the applicability of these materials to your specific organizational needs. Laws are subject to change at any time and legal requirements vary from jurisdiction to jurisdiction. Nothing herein should be relied upon without a full legal review of your organizational circumstances, as well as the laws of the operative jurisdiction. If you need warranted legal advice, see an attorney.

Disk Instructions

Included with your copy of *Best Practices* is a PC-type computer disk containing the sample policies from this handbook. Three separate files correspond to each of the tracks found within the handbook — Creative Agency, By the Book Agency and Leading Edge. Each track is saved as a plain ASCII text file, as well as a rich text format file, for use in any standard word processor software. *You may use, edit, copy and distribute these policies within your organization only. All copyright and credit information must remain intact. Any further distribution, in print or electronic format, is strictly prohibited.*

Support Services

The electronic version of *Best Practices* is provided to you as a courtesy. No formal customer support is offered, but questions about its use can be addressed to:

The Management Center
Consulting Services
870 Market Street, #800
San Francisco, CA 94110
tmc@tmcenter.org
(415) 362-9735, ext. 117

Most current Macintosh computers can read the PC-type disk supplied. But agencies wishing a Macintosh-style disk should send their original disk, plus $5 for shipping and handling, to the above address. Please allow 2-4 weeks for processing.

The Management Center, for an additional fee, can provide experienced consulting services in further customizing your personnel policies. Please call (415) 362-9735, ext. 127 for information.